BRISTOL
Derby DAYS

BRISTOL
Derby DAYS

By Neil Palmer
Foreword by John Ward

This edition first published in the UK in 2009
By Green Umbrella Publishing

© Green Umbrella Publishing 2009

www.gupublishing.co.uk

Publishers Jules Gammond and Vanessa Gardner

Creative Director: Kevin Gardner

Printed and bound by Cromwell Press Group

ISBN: 978-1-906635-85-5

My only regret in the writing of this book is that I never got to meet and spend time with the two greatest players ever to grace the city of Bristol. Their names run through the pages of the book and they are held, quite rightly, in high esteem by both Bristol City and Bristol Rovers and their supporters, and always will be.

This is why I dedicate a book about the Bristol derby to Geoff Bradford and John Atyeo. Gentlemen on and off the field, their like will never be seen again.

Contents

Foreword

It's a great honour to be asked to write a foreword for a book on both Bristol clubs. I feel privileged to have been asked to manage both Bristol Rovers and Bristol City in the same decade. Not only that but I am now made to feel very welcome at both clubs when I have had occasion to visit on business with opposing teams or an invitation to reminisce about old times.

The city lends itself very well to two very highly rated football league clubs who have enjoyed and endured different times in their rich histories. Names of individuals such as John Atyeo and Geoff Bradford sit comfortably with modern day heroes such as Marcus Stewart who has the distinction of playing for both clubs.

The rivalry is fierce during local derby days and the build-up to these fixtures excludes all other games some weeks prior to the big one. The result afterwards determines who goes to the pub and who goes to the off licence to drink indoors. Whatever happens, the rest of the football world closes down whilst the red and blue fight it out on their respected pitches. Above all else the strength and passion for their colours shows little equal in the game. In Bristol you have to be blue or red. To wear any other shirt is not allowed or tolerated. What it all means is that Bristol is the hotbed of league football in the West Country and long may it continue.

Having worn both colours I was very proud to be called an honorary Bristolian during my periods in the city. Good luck to you all and I know this book offers good memories and, of course, will provoke passionate discussions. Neil has a lot to answer for with his stories; provocation of views will be enjoyed by all colours and is his responsibility.

Good Luck
Enjoy

John Ward

Introduction

I'm sure when Bristol South End beat Eastville Rovers 2-1 at St John's Lane, Bedminster in 1894 they had no idea what they had started.

I decided to write this book as somebody who has lived in Bristol for the majority of his life and I'm extremely proud to live in a city that, to quote a good old Bristolian saying, has a "proper" derby.

Football fans will always talk about the Liverpool, Manchester, Glasgow and Birmingham derbies, even Sheffield gets mentioned although nationally it may not have the glamour of the others. But experience the build-up and atmosphere of the Bristol derby and you will realise it lacks nothing the others have. It splits a city and evokes a passion, loyalty, and rivalry that stands shoulder to shoulder with any derby in the world.

In a time when the modern game relies on stars from overseas and pays them in a week what the average fan couldn't earn in a year, I hope a nostalgic trip through 26 league and cup derbies from the post-war era will tell tales of local lads who became heroes and adopted players who will, to this day, be applauded by supporters for their contribution in the blue or red shirt. Hooper, Clark, Jarman, Cheesley, Randall, Newman, Phillips to name but a few; all with a tale to tell, and all having played their part in making the Bristol derby what it is today.

All the players in this book have given their time freely and they were a pleasure to interview. I have to be honest, the choice of players was fashioned by my own memories of past derbies and also by circumstance. There were some players I would have loved to interview for the book but they were either sadly no longer with us or in poor health. The players featured talk about how they came to arrive in the red shirt of City or the blue of Rovers, what the derby game meant to them and the derby match they remember most, for whatever reason. They also tell us where their careers went after playing for their respected clubs.

I am sure many fans will have their own classic, but these are the thoughts of the players. I hope the chapters will bring back some great memories, and of course not so great, for both sets of supporters. If you don't agree with the choice of players that's the beauty of football, it's all about opinions.

The most important thing is I hope you enjoy it.

Peter Hooper

How's that left foot?

FA Cup Fifth Round

15/02/1958

Bristol City	3-4	Bristol Rovers
Watkins 5 mins		Sykes 28 mins
Etheridge 67 mins		Ward 31 mins
Burden 70 mins		Meyer 42 mins
		Bradford 82 mins

HT 1-3
Att 39,126

Bristol City: Anderson, Terris, Thresher, Emery, Williams, Burden, Hinshelwood, Walker, Atyeo, Etheridge, Watkins.

Bristol Rovers: Nicholls, Bamford, Watling, Sykes, Pyle, Sampson, Petherbridge, Meyer, Bradford, Ward, Hooper.

Mention to any "gas" head who saw him play the name Pete Hooper and I bet you will get one of two replies "what a left foot" or "should've played for England". Pete was the lad from Teighnmouth who terrorised most full-backs put in front of him.

After playing for Kenya whilst doing national service, he was signed on his return by Bert Tann in 1953 without even seeing him play. Pete's reputation was good enough for Bert.

"He came to my mum and dad's house in Teighnmouth and said he had heard good things about me and would I sign. So I went up to Bristol and signed for a £10 signing on fee and I made my debut in front of 20,000 people in a 1-0 home win against Rotherham."

Four years later Pete, who was a regular for Rovers, was knocking on England's door. He found himself in what some Bristol football fans regard as the greatest local derby ever, a fifth round tie at Ashton Gate.

"I remember the Cup draw. I always wanted Blackpool home or away so I could play against my idol Stanley Matthews but when we were pitched against Bristol City I couldn't wait. We always had a good relationship with the City players; in fact, me, Barry Meyer and a couple of the lads would go and watch City at Ashton Gate if we didn't have a match. We would get stick off the fans but it was all good humoured.

"In preparation for the Cup game we stayed in Dawlish for the week prior to the match; this was a routine

we had for every Cup tie. It would be a week of hard training with Bert Tann and Fred Ford, his assistant, putting us through our paces and after training we would relax by playing snooker, cards or table tennis at the hotel.

"The crowd as we arrived on the bus was amazing with people cheering and clapping. Ashton Gate was almost at bursting point; you could really see what it meant to the fans of both sides. I remember being sat in the dressing room waiting to go out and Fred Ford coming over to me and telling me that he had heard City's young Scottish full-back Jim Terris was very nervous about facing me today, but to be honest I didn't think much of it.

"As we kicked off, the ball came to me and I controlled it. Terris backed off and seemed petrified. I pushed past him, dropped the shoulder and left him for dead and got a good cross in.

"I knew then I was going to have a good day. You have to realise in those days as soon as you got the ball, the opposing full-back would hit you as hard as he could to let you know he was there and more importantly, to see what you were made of, so as you can imagine when I saw him back off, that suited me fine."

It was a cagey start for both clubs but against the run of play City took the lead in the fifth minute when Wally Hinshelwood went down the line and sent over a perfect cross. John Watkins timed his run to perfection and headed past the groping Nicholls in the Rovers goal to put City one goal up.

"I have to admit the City goal really gave us a kick up the backside and as a result I started to get the ball more."

On the 28th minute, Terris was preparing to pass back to City keeper Anderson when Dai Ward darted in front of him. Terris tried to turn inside and Hooper took the ball off him and pushed it to Barry Meyer who then passed to Sykes and with great composure he unleashed a shot to the top corner to pull Rovers level. Rovers got more and more on top and on the 31st minute they went ahead. A cross from George Petherbridge, who was having quite a game against City hard man Mike Thresher on the right wing, was met by Geoff Bradford and City keeper Anderson. The ball fell to Dai Ward and he made it 2-1 to the "gas".

"At this point we were all over them. I was on fire on the left and Dai Ward was having a great game in the middle of the park; our defence was really solid keeping Atyeo at bay."

Rovers' possession came up trumps again in the 42nd minute when Hooper picked up the ball in his own half and set off on a trademark run, dribbling around two or three defenders before unleashing that left foot. Anderson pulled off a great save but pushed it to Barry Meyer who volleyed it home. City looked dead and buried, not just because they were 3-1 down, but because Rovers were playing so well; they looked like they could get five or six. Just before half-time City got a lifeline, Watkins was tripped by Sykes in the box and referee Reg Leafe pointed to the spot. Watkins got up off the floor to take it. He ran up and blasted it but Nicholls saved it.

"When Nicholls saved it I knew it was going to be our day and I think the crowd did too. We went into the dressing room at half-time on cloud nine but still relieved at the penalty miss. Bert Tann was never one

to heap praise on us but he told us to keep going and he thought we would get a few more.

"I don't know if it was a case of us taking our foot off the gas and thinking we had already won it or just City thinking they had nothing to loose but we were in for a tough second half."

On the 67th minute a mistake by Sykes put the ball at Etheridge's feet and he reacted with a long shot past Nicholls. Then on the 70th minute Burden went up to support the attack and a Rovers clearance bounced off of his chest and into the net.

"I couldn't believe how City had fought back. I was a virtual spectator out on the wing and had hardly touched the ball when City went 3-3. I honestly thought they would win."

With eight minutes remaining of what was a tremendous match Emery lost the ball to Ward who headed for goal. He passed to Bradford who was on the right and with City claiming offside Bradford fired the winner under Anderson's body and booked Rovers a place in the sixth round.

"At the final whistle to be honest I was relieved we had hung on in the second half and just snatched it. We celebrated with a cup of tea and when it all sank in I had mixed emotions about the game. It really was a game of both halves for me; I was on fire the first half but I didn't get a kick second half. Still, I was in the sixth round and I had been part of a game that did Bristol proud and is still talked about today."

Rovers drew Fulham in the next round at Craven Cottage but went out 2-1 with Geoff Bradford scoring Rovers' goal.

Pete was at Rovers until 1962. He scored 107 goals in 321 appearances.

"A lot of people ask me why I left Rovers and to be honest I just couldn't take Bert Tann's management style anymore. In all the games I've played for Rovers, he never once said 'Well done Pete'. A lot of rubbish was written about me wanting more money, in fact I was ready to walk away from football I was so fed up. Then Cardiff City offered me a lifeline and I grabbed it."

Pete moved to Cardiff City where he became a fans favourite and fulfilled his boyhood ambition of playing against a 51-year-old Stanley Matthews in a match against Stoke City at Ninian Park. Despite doing well for Cardiff, Pete returned to Bristol and joined Bristol City in 1963, but after serious illness he never recaptured the form of old and later joined non-league Worcester City. Pete left football and had various jobs including publican, prison officer and probation officer.

So what of the likeable Devonian now?

"I'm back in Devon and have two daughters and although I lost my wife recently I'm enjoying life. Rovers will always be my club and it was a privilege to put on the blue and white quarters. I get to some of the home games and the club are very good to me. The fans are always brilliant and the older ones always ask me about the Cup match. I still get the odd 'gas' head shouting 'Oi Pete, how's that left foot?'."

Brian Clark

Out of my father's shadow

Gloucester Cup

01/05/1962

Bristol City	3-1	Bristol Rovers
Clark 57, 63, 76 mins		Williams 42 mins

HT 0-1
Att 9,201

Bristol City: Cook, Ford, Smith, Etheridge, Connor, Casey, Peters, Clark, Tait, Williams, Derrick.

Bristol Rovers: Hall, Bradford, Hillard, Sykes, Frowen, Bumpstead, Jarman, Hamilton, Williams, Jones, Hooper.

There isn't much Bristol City and Cardiff City fans agree on but there is one thing: how good Brian Clark was. When Brian made his debut for Bristol City against Brentford in 1960 he fulfilled a boyhood ambition of playing for his local club. It was to be the start of a career that would take the likeable Bristolian into the hearts of both sets of fans.

"I always wanted to be a professional footballer. My nan used to take me to watch my dad play at Ashton Gate and afterwards I would get the players' autographs."

Brian's dad was the legendary Bristol City forward, Don Clark, who terrorised defenders in the 1940s. To this day, Don still holds City's goalscoring record of 41 goals in a season and in that 1946/47 season Clark senior missed five games through injury, so that will tell you the quality of stock Brian came from. Obviously being the son of a Bristol City player made Brian popular with his peers, but in 1957 he and 10 team mates would be the toast of every Bristol school child.

"I was in the Bristol Boys under 15's side and we played Swansea in the final of the national schools shield in a two legged final. We had 23,000 for the first leg at Ashton Gate where we won 5-0 and in the return, 11,000 were at the Vetch Field in Swansea where we won again 4-3 and won the shield 9-3 on aggregate. We had a great team with people like Jantzen Derrick, Adrian Williams and Peter Prewitt; although only a few went on to play in the professional ranks. A few days after the game we were given a reception by the Lord Mayor of Bristol and he gave all the schools in Bristol an extra day's holiday as a mark of our achievements."

It was a natural progression that Brian would sign for Bristol City, which he did in 1960, and made his debut in a 3-0 win against Brentford.

"It was fantastic to be playing with my idol John Atyeo who got a hat-trick in the game. I learnt so much from being with him. He was a true gent both on and off the field.

"My favourite derby memory was my hat-trick in the Gloucester Cup game in the 1961/62 season."

It was Rovers who took the lead on that warm May night just before half-time after a mistake from Tony Cook. James sent Keith Williams away on the left. As he crossed the ball, Tony Cook, in the City goal, let the ball run past him and it went into the net stunning the Ashton Gate crowd. Five minutes later, Rovers nearly went 2-0 up when Harold Jarman missed a sitter from six yards out after a pass from Williams.

"First half they were all over us. We just couldn't seem to get going."

But the second half belonged to one man: Brian Clark.

On 57 minutes Jantzen Derrick raced past Bradford to pull the ball back for Williams who in turn flicked it backwards for Clark to hammer the ball home from eight yards. Six minutes later a Peter's corner was met by Clark in the air and he sent the ball crashing into the Rovers net. Rovers were collapsing like a pack of cards and for a team who ruled the first half they were just hanging on. Clark completed his hat-trick in the 76th minute with a wonder goal: Derrick took a corner on the left, Etheridge headed towards goal, but Bradford headed it back out of the box only for Clark to meet the ball on the volley and crash it into the net.

"The final whistle was mayhem. I needed a police escort just to find my way off the pitch. The City fans were going crazy. I loved every minute of it; I don't even think I collected the ball."

Brian continued to score regularly for City and gradually lost the tag of being "Don Clark's son" and started to make his own name in the game.

"I was so proud to be the son of Don Clark and to see how people loved him, but I must admit when I started it was always Don Clark's son Brian and at times that did get me down. I was desperate to break out of my father's shadow and I felt I did that towards the end of my time at City."

Then in 1966, the first year after John Atyeo's departure, Bristol City manager Fred Ford made the decision to sell Brian to Huddersfield as part of a deal that involved midfielder John Quigley joining City – a decision at the time City fans thought was crazy and still do to this day. Brian had scored 80 goals in nearly 200 games at Ashton Gate.

"When John retired I thought I could take up where he left off but I wasn't given the chance. I didn't really have a say in the transfer. Admittedly I wasn't in the best of form but as would be proved later, whoever I played for I scored goals for them. Fred Ford made it clear I had no future at Ashton Gate. Unbeknown to me, Cardiff City and Swindon Town came in with bids for me but Fred Ford didn't want me to sign for local rivals and never told me of their interest."

After a brief spell at Huddersfield, Brian moved to Cardiff City in 1967 and became a big hit with the bluebird fans.

"I would've walked to Cardiff at the time to join them. I was in and out of the side at Huddersfield and wasn't wanted. Then Jimmy Scoular, the Cardiff manager, said he wanted me and that's all a player needs to hear. I made my debut against Derby County; we won 4–2 and I scored twice. I thought, what a start. I was also excited at the prospect of playing in Europe with Cardiff in the Cup Winners' Cup, Cardiff's path being through winning the Welsh Cup which they did on many occasions. I played in some fantastic stadiums all over Europe and I built up a great partnership with John Toshack up front."

It was in one such European tie that Brian cemented his name in the history of Cardiff City for ever more. The 1970/71 season Cardiff City drew Real Madrid in the Cup Winners' Cup quarter-final with the first leg being at Ninian Park and a crowd of 52,000 saw a Brian Clark goal beat the Spaniards 1-0.

"It was a hell of a night. Everyone was ecstatic and the crowd were amazing. I will never forget it."

Unfortunately for Cardiff City, the dream ended in the return leg when City lost 2-0 and went out 2-1.

Brian left Cardiff City in 1972. He had scored 75 goals in 182 games. He later went on to play for Bournemouth, Millwall and Newport County, and eventually hung up his boots in 1980 and went on to work as a rep.

"Today I live in Whitchurch in Cardiff and spend my days playing golf and chasing the grandchildren around. I still get to both Bristol City and Cardiff City games and get a great reception from both clubs and the fans, but Bristol City will always be my club."

Brian did break out of the shadow of his father and I think it's safe to say there are now two legends in the Clark family.

Howard Radford

I wondered if football was that important

League Division Two

01/11/1958

Bristol Rovers	**1-2**	**Bristol City**
Sykes 82 mins		*Tindill 68 mins*
		Atyeo 75 mins

HT 0-0
Att 32,102

Bristol Rovers: Radford, Doyle, Watling, Sykes, Pyle, Sampson, McIvenny, Biggs, Bradford, Ward, Hooper.

Bristol City: Cook, Hopkinson, Thresher, McCall, Williams, Burnden, Virgin, Tindill, Atyeo, Etheridge, Walker.

Being 15 minutes late for a trial game and letting in five goals is not the best of starts to a footballing career but that was the start of Howard Radford's love affair with Bristol Rovers. Born in Wales, Howard started playing football at 16 with his local club, Abercynon. After national service he played for Penrhiwceiber in the Welsh league and whilst playing for them he was spotted by Rovers' chief scout Wally Jennings.

"We were playing Cardiff City in the Welsh league and I got the time wrong and arrived 15 minutes late. At the end of the game, we had lost 5-0, so I was amazed when Wally came up to me and asked me to come and sign for Rovers."

Apparently Wally went straight to Bert Tann and told him he found a goalkeeper you could put straight in the first team. Although Howard wasn't the biggest of goalkeepers, around 5ft 10in, he was extremely brave – a part of his game that would later in his career cost him many appearances due to injury.

"I was 21 and Bert Tann picked me to play in a friendly against FC Haarlem from Holland. We drew 0-0 and to be honest, I didn't have a lot to do but I played well. I then made my league debut away against Southend in October 1951. We lost 2-1 but again I did OK. During my time at Rovers I played in a few Bristol derbies but the one I remember was the match straight after the death of my good friend and team mate Harry Bamford."

Harry Bamford was the ultimate professional. He played right-back for Rovers for his entire 13-year career from 1945 until his tragic death in 1958. He was killed on his way back from coaching the youngsters at Clifton College in Bristol. His motorcycle was in a collision with a van at Apsley Road in Clifton. He remained in hospital for three days before finally dying from his injuries on October 31st 1958. At the time of his death he was a regular in the team and had played the previous 59 consecutive games. Harry left a wife and child. It was a death that shook the whole of Bristol and it hit the footballing fraternity very hard. Bristol City chairman Harry Dolman said "He was a great man and will be sadly missed", Rovers' manager Bert Tann said of his death "A bit of Bristol Rovers has died with him", and so a Harry Bamford memorial fund was set up. On May 8th 1958 a combined City and Rovers team played Arsenal at Eastville and a crowd of 28,347 turned up to see the Bristol select side win 5-4, thus the Harry Bamford Trophy was introduced for a local footballer who had showed great sportsmanship.

"Harry was a great friend to me. I had lived with him in Montpelier for a couple of months and we struck up a great understanding on and off the pitch. He would head the ball back to me when we were defending corners and to know he had that much faith in me did my confidence the world of good. I will never forget when I heard he had the accident; someone told me at the club and I was just numb and when he died we were all in a terrible state. He died on the Friday and the fixtures had put us with a home game against Bristol City the next day. I thought this game can't go on. I wondered if football was that important and to be honest, I didn't really want to play."

But the game went ahead on the agreement of the clubs and the FA and a packed Eastville marked the passing of one of Bristol football's gentlemen.

"In the end I was glad the game went ahead as it gave the players and supporters the chance to show their respect. We had a minute's silence and we all wore black arm bands. The fans of both teams were superb and you could've heard a pin drop. I remember I had my head bowed and had my eyes shut just thinking of all the good times I had had with Harry on and off the pitch. As the whistle blew for the end of the silence I lifted my head, wiped away a tear, and got on with the game."

The game was a typical hard fought derby with both teams going close in the first half: Rovers with a fierce Geoff Bradford effort well saved by Cook in the City goal and City with a Tindill header that just went wide. The second half was a thunderous affair and City took the lead on the 68th minute when Cook sent a long ball down field. Atyeo outjumped Pyle of Rovers and the ball fell to Tindill who lobbed Radford in the Rovers goal.

"I thought Tindill was going to shoot and I had strayed off my line and when he lobbed me I was nowhere near it. City went further ahead on 75 minutes when Etheridge headed down a City centre from the right-wing and bad marking in the Rovers defence left Atyeo unmarked to tap in an empty net. The game looked dead and buried for Rovers but Sykes gave them a lifeline on 82 minutes when Dai Ward put him through to smash the ball past Cook and into the City goal. Rovers couldn't get back in the game despite a late effort from Ward and the game ended with a 2-1 victory for City.

"I think the occasion had got to us a bit. We made two bad mistakes and City punished us at the end of the game. We all shook hands and went back to the dressing room. It had been a very difficult day for all of us."

Howard went on to play 11 seasons and amassed around 486 games when he signed for the 12th season for Rovers, just after having his fifth operation on his knee.

"I sat at home and just thought that I've had enough. I went back to the club, saw Bert Tann, and told him. He shook my hand and wished me all the best."

Howard then became a publican and is now retired and lives in Chudleigh, Devon.

"I play golf and meet up with my old team mate Pete Hooper now and then who lives near me to reminisce about old times. Rovers were my only club. They are still in my heart and always will be. I had some of the best times of my life at the club but also one of the worst."

Geoff Merrick

A *born winner*

League Division Two

28/12/1974

Bristol Rovers	**1-4**	**Bristol City**
Fearnley 26 mins		*Fear 58, 90 mins*
		Mann 72 mins
		Tainton 77 mins

HT 1-0
Att 20,911

Bristol Rovers: Sheppard, Bater, Parsons, Aitken, Taylor, Prince, Fearnley, Coombes, Warboys, Staniforth, Britten, substitute: Jones.

Bristol City: Cashley, Sweeney, Drysdale, Mann, Collier, Merrick, Tainton, Ritchie, Fear, Cheesley, Durrell, substitute: Griffin.

Geoff Merrick has been involved in Bristol City's highest moment. He has also, unfortunately for him, been involved in their lowest. Although the latter, for many, is what they remember Geoff for, we must not forget what a tremendous servant this local lad was to the red half of the city. Born within a stones throw of Ashton Gate the young Geoff was taken by his father to watch both City and Rovers.

"My dad would take me to Rovers or City even though we lived near the City ground, it didn't matter as long as I could watch football. At that time I had two loves: football and tractors, and it's funny how in my life I ended up making a career with both of them."

Geoff was chased by many clubs as a youngster including both Bristol clubs as well as Liverpool and Aston Villa but he decided to sign for the club down the road.

"I remember signing. I got to meet the great John Atyeo who shook my hand and welcomed me to the club. It was 1966 and just after I played for England schoolboys against West Germany which is an honour very dear to me to this day. It was such a different era then I would walk to games carrying my own boots and I loved it at the club."

Geoff continued to make great progress in the City ranks alternating between left-back and central-defender and although not that big for a defender, he possessed every attribute required for that roll. He was strong, brave, tackled powerfully, had great timing in the air and read the game well, so it wasn't long before he was picked for the first team.

"I had done well as a youngster at City and played in the youth team and the reserves. It was there I first started to get some sort of feeling of a Bristol derby. We had played Rovers on many occasions and they were always hard, tough games and you never wanted to loose them as the whole club wanted you to win. Even the older pros would ask us how we got on. It meant a lot to me not just from a professional point of view, but as I came from Bristol I wanted at an early age to do well for the supporters."

Geoff's debut was against Aston Villa, he was 17 years old and although a few niggling injuries early on caused him to be in and out of the side, once he got a run in the team there was no looking back for the talented young Bristolian and at 20 years of age he captained the club.

"To be made captain was a great honour for me. I was a local boy and it was a dream come true. Although I was only 20 I got great support from the lads and I really took to it. I enjoyed organising and being Alan Dicks' eyes and ears on the pitch."

And that relationship was never more prevalent than the Bristol derby in December 1974 at Eastville.

"I remember that match. The weather was awful. I remember chatting before the game to Alan regarding what would be the best way for us tactic wise to play. We decided with the wind so strong and it blowing from Tote End to Muller Road if we could keep their attacks to a minimum in the first half we could use the wind in the second to our advantage. So I told the lads we would play offside whenever we could first half and put up the field as often as possible and try not to let them out of their half. Although the conditions were awful it was a great atmosphere and just what you would expect from a derby match. Eastville was always a good ground when it was packed to the rafters."

City's plan started well but then on 26 minutes a shot from Rovers' Britten was parried out by Cashley and Fearnley pounced to put Rovers one goal up.

"I was livid. He was offside yet the ref gave it, still we had to get on with it and re-group. We went in 1-0 down at half-time and I knew that one goal would not be enough for Rovers and when we got going in the second half especially with 'cheese' and Keith up front we would be OK."

On 57 minutes City won a corner which Durrell drilled into the box.

"I just remember slicing at it as it went towards goal and typical Keith nipped in to get the equaliser. Then on 72 minutes Jimmy Mann beat Rovers keeper Dickie Sheppard on the near post and I knew we were home and dry. Rovers were having a torrid time in defence with the wind and they could hardly get out of their half. At the back, me and Gary Collier didn't have much to do so I would push up leaving Gary to do the marking. I remember winning the ball in midfield and pushing it to Trevor Tainton. He let fly and it crashed into the Rovers net, leaving poor old Dickie Sheppard stranded for our third goal. Then right at the end, Ray Cashley kicked a ball almost the length of the field and Keith volleyed it into the net for our fourth. At the whistle the City fans at the Muller Road End were jumping up and down and we went over to them to applaud them. As I walked off I said to the ref Gordon Hill that the Rovers goal was offside and he said 'I think you might be right', I just laughed but it would have been a different story had we lost 1-0."

Geoff's career at City went from strength to strength. In some papers he was referred to as the "Second Division's Bobby Moore" due to his cool head under pressure and ability to make things look so easy on the ball. It wasn't long before the mighty Arsenal were willing to offer to take the City captain to Highbury but the offer, rumoured to be around £275,000, was rejected by the City board. On 20th April 1976 City beat Portsmouth 1-0 at Ashton Gate to clinch promotion to Division One and the top flight of English football.

"It was a great feeling for all of us that night. We had worked so hard and had grown up as a team together and we had achieved what we set out to do and what some people thought wasn't possible.

"I will never forget the scenes in the Williams Stand as we looked out on those City fans. It was truely a great night to be a red and it got even better for City as they were due to play Arsenal at Highbury on the opening day of the 1976/77 season and after a wonderful performance by every one of them they came away the victors 1-0.

"I remember the whole of the motorway being red and white. It was like a Cup final and as we got to the ground I remember it was a lovely day and the sun just glinted off the roof at Highbury and to be honest I had to pinch myself. We got off the coach and walked into the marble hall entrance and I thought this is it, and as I ran out on that sunny afternoon that was the greatest moment of my footballing career. I was a Bristol lad leading out my local team at Highbury in the top flight of football and that will stay with me forever."

After City's good start to life at the top, manager Alan Dicks decided he wanted some more top flight experience in the side and that arrived at Ashton Gate in the shape of ex-Leeds United and England defender Norman Hunter. Geoff was moved out to left-back and Norman was central defence. Left-back was not Geoff's preferred position but he got on with it, even though the decision came as a bit of a surprise.

"I was surprised. I had been playing well consistently and left-back didn't feel as comfortable as in the centre but I just got on with it."

Hunter left after three years and Geoff reverted back to centre but he could not stop the club's decline on the pitch as they fell from Division One to Division Four in successive years. However, it was the financial decline of the club that would be one of Geoff's toughest battles.

"People often ask me if I had any inclination of the state of things behind the scenes and I can honestly say I did not. I had been out injured and was coming back from a reserve game at Aston Villa and as we arrived at Ashton Gate on the Saturday night we were met by Jimmy Mann in the players entrance. He had a scruffy ripped up old piece of paper in his hand with some names on it. Jim said he had been given these names by the directors and we had to report to the directors on Monday morning. We all had no idea why.

"When I look back, that one episode really sums up the shoddy way it was handled. The board couldn't even speak to us face to face, they gave an old bit of paper to another player to tell us. It really showed a lack of feeling by the club towards us.

"We arrived on the Monday: myself, Gerry Sweeney, Chris Garland, David Rogers, Peter Aitken, Trevor Tainton, Jimmy Mann, and Julian Marshall. We were told of the club's plight and that for City to survive we had to rip up our contracts to save the club as we were the top earners and if we didn't, the club would fold. We were put under immense pressure by the media and the club to make our decision. We called in

Gordon Taylor from the PFA and to be honest he was a waste of time – I got the feeling if we had been a bigger club maybe they would've fought a bit harder for us but as it was Fourth Division Bristol City players, nobody was interested. They didn't seem to realise that for the two weeks while we were deciding, we were fighting for our livelihoods and our careers. My friends and family were wonderful and my wife Wendy was a real rock to me, she was so strong and when we talk about it now she tells me how worried she was and how badly it affected the family. It really was a very unpleasant episode in mine and the club's history. We even offered to play for less money but there was no negotiation."

Geoff, along with the others, tore up their contracts and left the club with two weeks wages. He had played around 430 games for City and that day at Highbury couldn't have been further away as he now had to find work. Geoff and Chris Garland were offered the chance to go to Hong Kong to play for Carolina Hill for a few months which they accepted. Leaving their families behind, off they went.

"It was heartbreaking leaving the family but I had to provide for them. I had an offer from Portsmouth just before we went but I gave the people in Hong Kong my word I was going so it was too late for Pompey. People ask me if the couple of weeks turmoil at City affected me, well my playing weight was 11 stone and I boarded that plane to Hong Kong 9 stone so you can draw your own conclusions."

On Geoff's return some months later he had an offer from Norwich City but he decided to retire at 31 and played non-league football in and around Bristol whilst working on a farm and rediscovering his love for all things on the farm.

"When I was a kid I loved tractors and one of my teachers even wanted me to go to agricultural college and drop football. In pre-season at City I would work on a friend's farm to keep fit. Then while I was at the funeral of the talented Bristol Rovers player Micky Barratt, who tragically died of cancer aged 24, Rovers' manager David Williams asked where I was playing and if I would like to play a few games for the reserves to add a little experience to their young side and help the lads, so I said yes. I went and played for Rovers and loved every minute of it. Even though it was reserve football, I played at some great grounds that I thought I would never set foot in again. I was about 34 years old and had always been fit and I must admit I never thought I would put on the blue and white quarters but the club were very good to me."

Geoff played for Bath City, Yeovil, Bridgewater and Minehead and hung up his boots in his mid 40s.

"I never wanted to go into coaching; I always thought football is for playing."

Today Geoff lives on his farm just outside Bristol with his lovely wife where they not only tend to cattle and horses, but Geoff runs his commercial building company. I called Geoff's chapter "A born winner" and I know it's a term banded around quite frequently towards footballers today but I don't necessarily mean a winner in the trophy sense, although Geoff has his share, but a winner in what he has achieved when life puts an obstacle in the way. It's testimony to Geoff that he has made a success of his business outside football and not let the whole Ashton Gate episode cloud his life. Many City fans will have their own opinions on that time but we all should remember Geoff Merrick as the local captain who led out his team that sunny day at Highbury and gave around 15 years service to the reds, not as somebody caught up in the mismanagement of a football club.

Harold Jarman

Next thing I knew I was lying on the dog track

League Division Three

14/12/1963

Bristol Rovers	4-0	Bristol City
Bradford 4, 84 mins		
Jarman 9 mins		
Biggs 11 mins		

HT 3-0
Att 19,451

Bristol Rovers: Hall, Hilliard, Jones, Oldfield, Day, Mabbutt, Jarman, Brown, Biggs, Hamilton, Bradford.

Bristol City: Gibson, Briggs, Thresher, Parr, Connor, Llow, Derrick, Clark, Atyeo, Williams, Hooper.

If there was ever a poll to find Mr Bristol Rovers, Harold Jarman would be top or very near it. Throughout his illustrious career with the pirates he has played at every level for them, been youth team boss, reserve team boss and even manager. If you speak to him today, the wirey built winger of yesterday has lost nothing of his passion and enthusiasm for the game let alone his affection for Bristol Rovers.

Born in Bristol in 1939, the young Harold spent his early days kicking a ball with his brothers under the shadow of Ashton Gate at their home near Ashton Park. It was watching Bristol City that he got his first introduction to football.

"I would go to City with my brothers and my first recollection was watching them around 1944 against West Bromwich Albion. I don't remember the score but I do remember the crowd and the atmosphere even at that young age. I played for my local club Victoria Athletic. By today's standards I was late coming into football at 19 but I was doing an apprenticeship in carpentry so I was combining both.

"I then got a visit at home by Rovers' scout Wally Jennings. Looking back it was quite funny really. He turned up at the house and my dad was rummaging down the back of the settee for half a crown he had dropped. Wally came in and asked my dad if 'Harold would like to come to Rovers' and my dad replied 'What does he want to go to you lot for? He could play for Arsenal or Portsmouth' and Wally just went away."

Unperturbed, Harold continued with his goalscoring for Ashton Park and Wally turned up again at the family house. Not to be put off by Mr Jarman senior, Wally signed Harold on a part-time basis due to his apprenticeship.

"I remember playing in the colts team at Rovers and one of my first games was against Bristol City on the County Ground. I got kicked till kingdom come. I never realised what a step up in football it would be. It was a really big game, even at colt level, nobody took any prisoners. They were all Bristol kids and so were we and god did we want to win. The game ended 2-2 and I was black and blue when I came off."

After Harold's baptism of fire at colt level he moved up to the reserves and at the end of the season Fred Ford said to him that Bert Tann wanted to see him.

"I went to see Bert and he asked me to sign full time and I agreed on the spot and we shook hands. When I got home I told my dad and my mum and she asked me if it was a proper job. I laughed and told her it was about a pound more than a carpenter so she was pleased."

Harold made his debut against Swansea Town on December 26th 1959 in a 3-1 win in front of 17,000 at Eastville. Harold's career took off from there.

"I had made my mark in the first team and things went well and I remember crossing swords with City on many occasions but the match I remember most was on 14th December 1963. It was a League Three game at Eastville and it was a full house. George Petherbridge who was retiring told me 'Harold, when you play against Mike Thresher never go on his outside, always cut in' and I remember thinking 'yeah yeah George'. Within minutes of the kick-off I got the ball and took on Mike and proceeded to drop the shoulder and go on his outside. With that I felt I had been hit by a steam train and the next thing I knew I was lying on the dog track. After I had picked myself up from the track and the resulting free kick, we pressed on and Ray Mabbutt struck a cracking shot which Mike Gibson in the City goal fumbled on the line, only for Geoff Bradford to tap it over and put us one up after four minutes. It didn't stop there. I picked up the ball on about nine minutes and I thought I will have a go and it went straight into the top corner. We were on fire and City were shell shocked."

It got worse for the robins two minutes later when Alfie Biggs hit a stunning volley which crashed past the helpless Gibson.

City and their supporters couldn't believe it. They had hardly had a kick and were three down with only 11 minutes gone. Rovers went close again and could have made it four just before half-time.

"As we went off at half-time we knew we were going to win and City just seemed in a daze. I do remember Mike Thresher shouting to them 'Right lads kick them second half'. Mike was a really hard man but also a very good player. I just think he was trying to get some reaction from his team mates."

The second half failed to be as lively as the first with City having nothing to loose and they pushed Rovers back into their own half with Atyeo and Derrick going close but nothing came of it. Just before the end, Rovers' Hamilton gained space down the right and he placed a superb ball right on to Bradford's head for Rovers' fourth and Bradford's second, for the blue half of Bristol to go into raptures.

"I loved the derby matches and a lot of the City players were friends of mine but once the game kicked off we were enemies for 90 minutes. The games were hard but never nasty."

In the summer of 1972, Don Megson arrived as manager and obviously wanted his own players. Harold who was now 33 found himself in and out of the side. Then an offer from Newport County came in for regular first team football so Harold left. He had played over 450 games for the club and scored 127 goals.

"I was gutted to leave Rovers as I did feel I had a couple of years left in me but it wasn't to be."

After a season at Newport County, Harold went to the USA to play for the New York Cosmos.

"It came about due to a contact I had and they looked after me. It was just before Pelé and Besty went there so football was just taking off but I knew it was never going to be long term. When I returned to Bristol I played in and around the local football scene and then got a job at Bristol Rovers as the youth team boss under Bobby Campbell. It was a great job. The crop of kids we had at that time were unbelievable; it was around 1977 and it was a joy to come to work."

After a successful time as youth boss, Harold was made up to reserve team boss and then in 1979 Bobby Campbell got the sack and the board offered the job to Harold.

"I have very few regrets in my life but taking the Rovers job was one. I should've left with Bobby. I didn't feel I was backed by the board and didn't feel I had their support. If we got a 1-1 draw away I would hear directors saying we were lucky and I just thought they could have been more supportive to me and the team."

Harold was replaced in April 1980 by Terry Cooper. His record in charge was played 24, won 7, drew 9 and lost 8.

"I didn't feel my record was bad but that's football. I'm only pleased the spell in charge didn't spoil my relationship with the fans as that can happen when ex-players take charge of their old club."

Today Harold still lives in Bristol and is retired. He plays golf and takes his grandchildren to Rovers.

"I love going back. The fans are fantastic to me and they always have been. I can't sing their praises enough. Throughout my career, I always felt I had their support and I hope they realised what that blue and white quartered shirt meant to me."

Donnie Gillies

All I *wanted to do was play*

Gloucester Cup Final

15/05/1979

Bristol Rovers	0-2	Bristol City
		Mann 55 mins
		Gow 79 mins

HT 0-0
Att 6,661

Bristol Rovers: Thomas, Palmer, Bater, Aitken, Taylor, Williams, Emmanuel, Mabbutt, Petts, White, Brown, substitutes: Clark, Griffiths.

Bristol City: Shaw, Gillies, Whitehead, Gow, Sweeney, Merrick, Tainton, Ritchie, Royle, Mabbutt, Mann, substitutes: Penny, Cormack.

If Donnie Gillies was playing today his worth to Bristol City would be measured in the millions. A goalscorer who could play up front, midfield and in defence. In fact if it wasn't for his versatility he would've scored more goals and certainly played more games for the reds. But in a time when one substitute was allowed, manager Alan Dicks went into many games with Donnie on the bench just in case the versatile Scotsman was needed in any area of the pitch. When called to do so this hard tackling, no-nonsense Scot would give everything for the City cause, and his enthusiasm and passion for the game has never dwindled to this day.

Born in Glencoe, Scotland, Donnie learnt the art of goalscoring at Inverness Clachnacuddin in the Highland league and it wasn't long before he came to the attention of Morton in the Scottish league.

"I continued to score for Morton and we came down for a brief tour in England and played a few games against Portsmouth, Hereford, Swindon and Bristol City. I had done really well and scored in every game and that's when unbeknown to me, Bristol City got interested. Months went by and Morton were playing Celtic away. We were 2-0 up at half-time and I got the two goals so as you can imagine I was dumbfounded when I was substituted at half-time. It was very near to transfer deadline day and I was given a ticket to Heathrow and was told to go to Glasgow Airport the following day. At Heathrow I would be met by a club representative and I swear to god I had no idea what was going on. Waiting for me at Heathrow was Ken Wimshurst who was Bristol City's assistant manager, and that's when I realised I was going to Bristol City. It's amazing when I look back at it."

So after Donnie's initial shock, he signed for £30,000 in March 1973 and made his debut against Nottingham Forest away in a 1-0 defeat – a game that saw the winner scored by ex-City forward John Galley.

"I remember that game. I was hit in the first five minutes by the Forest centre-half and my god I thought I had been hit by a truck and I remember thinking 'welcome to the English league'. I was also gutted as City had just sold Galley to Forest and kept Bobby Gould. I wish it was the other way round as I had bundles of pace and it would have been great to have played off a big man like Galley. But Gouldy was a different sort of player and we never really gelled on or off the pitch."

Donnie's career took off at Bristol City but he increasingly found himself playing everywhere on the pitch.

"When I was a kid, I would play everywhere and that's what happened at City and maybe I was stupid not to put my foot down but all I wanted to do was play. I remember one week I played Arsenal on the Saturday at right-back then St.Mirren in the Anglo Scottish Cup on the Wednesday night where I was centre-forward and midfield on the following Saturday at Manchester United but as I said, I just got on with it.

"My memories of games with the Rovers are quite vivid. I recall going to Eastville while I was out injured watching us beat Rovers 4-1 when Keith Fear scored two goals. I think it was the 1974 derby. I was in the crowd with a few mates and I nearly got lynched by the Rovers fans, which was a bit hairy.

"The game I remember most was a Gloucester Cup final at Eastville. I had been out of the side for months with a torn thigh muscle which caused me all sorts of problems. It was the end of the season and the club were going to America for our club tour and I was desperate to go but Alan Dicks said that I couldn't cos I wasn't fit enough. So I worked hard with Les Bardsley, the physiotherapist, and I said I was fit to play. Alan put me in and I remember after the first couple of minutes Rovers' Phil Bater hit me like an express train. Now Phil was a lovely bloke but my god he was hard. After that challenge the leg was fine so I knew it would be OK throughout the game."

The match at Eastville was a typical hard fought derby. The two teams were in different leagues: Bristol City were in Division One and Bristol Rovers in Division Two. The City side was full of experience and Rovers fielded five teenagers including 17-year-old Gary Mabbutt, the son of Rovers legend Ray Mabbutt and brother of City's Kevin Mabbutt, who was also playing. It would be the first time the brothers had met in a Bristol derby game. City were the better side in the first half going close with a Jimmy Mann free kick that was superbly saved by Thomas in the Rovers goal. Thomas saved them again after a Joe Royle header was pushed round the post by the young Welshman.

The teams went in level at half-time with City regretting their finishing, but then 10 minutes after the interval Jimmy Mann found space and hit a low shot to put City 1-0 up. This sparked Rovers into life and Paul Petts went past City's Clive Whitehead and crossed for Steve White to head home but the ball was cleared off the line by Gillies. With Rovers trying desperately to get back in the game, City's Gerry Gow picked up the ball with 10 minutes to go and his 30-yard drive gave Thomas in the Rovers goal no chance to stop the score from being 2-0 to City.

"I loved playing in local derbies. I knew what it meant to the fans and how much it meant to us players.

At that time it was like two derby games: not only was it City and Rovers, but our City team had loads of Scottish lads in and Rovers were full of Welsh so it really spiced the game up."

With the win over Rovers and the good news that his torn thigh muscle was OK, Donnie got himself ready for the American tour when there was a knock on his door.

"This guy was standing there and he told me he was from the department of health and social security so I told him to come on in. He hands me a copy of the Evening Post match report on the derby game and says 'What's that?',
I said 'What?',
He replied 'You played in the week and you have been claiming dole money for 16 weeks.'
I said 'The club has claimed sick money while I was out injured for 16 weeks which they are entitled to do and they have that money deducted from wages.'
So he got a bit flustered and told me 'Well, you didn't tell us you were playing Thursday night and you owe us about £1.32.'
So I laughed, gave him the money and threw him out of the house. As he was running down my road he shouted 'Up the gas!'
So that was my memory of that Rovers derby."

Donnie went on to be part of a great Bristol City side and always enjoyed a great rapport with the City fans. But a phone call while he was out playing skittles changed everything.

"I came home and my late wife told me Rovers manager, Terry Cooper, had phoned and asked if I wanted to play football for him. I assumed it was a charity match, but then I had a call first thing in the morning from the gaffer, Alan Dicks, who asked me if I had spoken to Terry Cooper.
I said 'No.'
He replied 'Well he wants to sign you for the Rovers.'
I said 'I can't go to the Rovers.'
Alan replied 'Donnie you have to go. If you don't you won't play for City again as we can't pay you.'
So that's how I ended up at Rovers, because of my five year contract at City I had become too expensive and it was the fall out of the money problems the club would face. I thought long and hard how I would be received and I knew I would get stick but it was a job and I was a professional."

Donnie had played 217 games for City and scored 30 goals. So he signed for £50,000 in June 1980 and made his debut in the blue and white quarters in a 1-1 draw at home to Leyton Orient.

"To be fair, the Rovers fans were very good to me and when I look back at my two seasons at the club, on the field, things went well. I played in two more derbies against City which was very strange but as matches they were awful 0-0 draws but off the field it was probably the most traumatic time for the Rovers as a club. The stand at Eastville burnt down, so they then moved to Ashton Gate and eventually to Twerton, so it was a very difficult time for everyone at the club. Terry Cooper left and Bobby Gould took over as manager. I had a feeling Bobby was going to be manager but we never saw eye to eye when we were both at City so the writing was on the wall for me and it became even clearer when he never picked me. I remember being on the training pitch with Dario Gradi who was helping Bobby out. He was a tremendous coach as he has proved over the years and he is also a lovely man. He asked if I was injured as he couldn't believe I wasn't in the side again but Bobby made it personal. I think it was because he realised I was earning more money than he was. Things then came to a head and Rovers paid off my contract and I left and dropped into non-

league with Bath City, Yeovil Town, Gloucester City and Paulton Rovers."

Today, Donnie lives with his second wife in their beautiful cottage outside Glastonbury. He runs his own successful fruit and veg business which he has done for many years.

"My kids are all grown up and I'm enjoying life. I still see some of the City lads and when we meet up it's like we have never been apart. City were always my club but I do feel privileged to have played for both clubs, not many have."

Stuart Taylor

A Rovers great

FA Cup Third Round Replay

30/01/1968

Bristol Rovers	1-2	Bristol City
Taylor 28 mins		Crowe 38 mins
		Galley 40 mins

HT 1-2
Att 30,157

Bristol Rovers: Taylor, Hillard, Munro, Williams, Taylor, Stone, Jarman, Jones, Plumb, Mabbutt, Jones, substitute: Ronaldson.

Bristol City: Gibson, Parr, Briggs, Wimshurst, Connor, Bush, Derrick, Crowe, Galley, Quigley, Peters, substitute: Garland.

There are not many gas heads that saw the young Stuart Taylor play who'd predict he would go on to have an illustrious career at the Rovers, let alone break the appearance record. Eastville was certainly split in those early days regarding the tall young defender. Some say given time he would make the grade whilst others thought he just wasn't up to it but the most important thing of all was that one man in the pro-Taylor camp was manager Bert Tann.

Taylor grew up in Bristol and as a boy was taken regularly by his father to Ashton Gate to watch Bristol City.

"It seems funny now but yes my dad was a strong City fan and we went every week in the early days. They were my club. I do remember my mates nagging me to go to the Rovers with them and I think my reply was something like 'you have to be joking', but after wearing me down, I went. I was about 15 I think and Rovers were playing Leeds United. They went a goal down then won 5-1 with Geoff Bradford scoring twice and Pete Hooper scoring. I always remember that game. The atmosphere and the crowd were awesome."

Stuart was captain of Bristol Boys and signed for Bristol City whilst doing his apprenticeship as a plumber but he never played.

"I was at City for two years but nothing really happened and I never got a game so in the end I just thought, 'sod it, I'm off', and I left and went and played for Hanham Athletic. Rovers then stepped in and asked me to play for them on a part-time basis as I was working. I made my Rovers debut against Workington away, we drew 1-1 and in those days we went by train to matches. I remember getting back to Bristol at 4am and going to work at 8am so when Rovers offered me a full-time contract I was very happy. I had finished my apprenticeship so it worked out well for me and the club.

"I never really played that many games against City as we were often in different divisions but I do remember a couple. In the Gloucester Cup match in 1969 at Eastville, we were 0-0 at half-time and City came out second half and put five past us. Garland, Derrick, Galley, Kellard, and Skirton all scored. It was the whole of the City forward line, they were fantastic the second half and we couldn't get near them. The other game is the Cup tie and subsequent replay 1968 third round. The first game was at Ashton Gate and the big build-up was me, the youngster, and how I would fare against John Galley if he played as he was out injured. They eventually brought him back for the tie. John was a seasoned professional and I have to say I rated him as good as John Atyeo so I knew I would be up against it. As it turned out, 37,000 fans at Ashton Gate witnessed a terrible 0-0. The game was awful. If it had been in your back garden you would've shut the curtains. Depite this I had a really good game but knew we would have to be on top form to beat them at Eastville."

With 30,000 crammed into Eastville under the floodlights, Rovers took on City in the replay. Rovers started brightly and although they were without front man Alfie Biggs through injury, they attacked from the kick-off and in the fifth minute Ray Mabbutt swept inside and hit a great shot that Gibson in the City goal saved well. On the 27th minute City's Briggs gave away a free kick, Doug Hillard lofted the ball high into the City box and after a scramble the ball went for a corner. Jones crossed the ball into the box and Gibson punched it out but only to Williams and his resulting chip back towards goal was met by the young Taylor who turned the ball into City's net.

"I couldn't believe it! I didn't score many and the ones I did were usually with my head. The crowd went crazy. The feeling as I ran back to defence and the other players' reaction will always stay with me."

Although Rovers were on top, the lead didn't last long and 10 minutes later Crowe whipped a pass to Peters who then returned it to Crowe and he drove a shot past Taylor, the Rovers keeper, to net the equaliser.

With the Muller Road End an ecstatic sea of red and white, Jantzen Derrick crossed a dangerous ball into the Rovers box and John Galley lost his marker, Taylor, and buried the ball into the top corner to put City 2-1 up at half-time. Rovers came out fighting in the second half and after some good work by Mabbutt, City's Gordon Parr headed off the line. On the 57th minute, Rovers' Plumb found space and his shot crashed against the City post. Rovers threw everything at City and with a last gasp, Williams let fly after some good work from Hillard, resulting in a shot hitting the woodwork and so with the whistle blown, Rovers were out but my god what a fight.

"I had mixed feelings at full time. I was pleased with my goal but felt I had let the lads down for the winner. That's how good Galley was, if you gave him a chance he would score."

Taylor came out of the game full of credit. The Bristol Evening Post described him in their match review as a "gigantic, powerful star for the Rovers".

And so that star who was taken as a youngster by his dad to watch Bristol City, went on to play over 600 games for the gas and on March 11th 1980 Taylor played his last game at home against Preston North End.

"I was 33 and to be honest I felt I could've played a few more seasons. It looked like Harold Jarman would get the Rovers job and he said if he got it he would give me another season but Terry Cooper got it and I just didn't figure in his plans. So I ended up leaving on a free transfer and the opportunity came up to join Chelsea but I opted to go to Bath City where I ended up as manager. After a couple of seasons at Twerton I went out of football and now run my own plumbing business which I enjoy. I go to every Rovers home match and the supporters are brilliant. They always say when Rovers get a corner 'you going up Stu?' so the response I get is fantastic."

Will Taylor's record of over 600 games for one club ever be broken? In the modern game I don't think so. This likeable Bristolian will always be in any list of Rovers greats. After a shaky start he won over the Tote End and you couldn't get a better recommendation than that.

Paul Cheesley

What if...?

League Division Two

30/08/1975

Bristol City	**1-1**	**Bristol Rovers**
Cheesley 19 mins		Bannister 3 mins

HT 1-1
Att 17,918

Bristol City: Cashley, Sweeney, Drysdale, Gow, Collier, Merrick, Tainton, Ritchie, Mann, Cheesley, Brolly, substitute: Gillies.

Bristol Rovers: Eadie, Smith, Williams, Aitken, Taylor, Prince, Stephens, Pulis, Warboys, Bannister, Evans, substitute: Fearnley.

If ever a player epitomised the uncertainty of the professional footballer, Paul Cheesley was that man. A local lad on his way to potentially being as big a hero of the Bristol City faithful as the great John Atyeo when a cruel twist of fate left him, and the red half of the City, wondering, what if...?

Born in Easton-in-Gordano, Bristol in 1953, Paul showed, even at 14, a tremendous self belief that unknown to him would be a vital commodity in his forthcoming career.

"I wrote to both City and Rovers as a kid and after seeing me play for my local team, Easton in Gordano boys club, they both asked me to sign as a schoolboy. I asked them what that meant and they told me one of the conditions was that I couldn't play for my local club anymore, so I told them no thanks and I walked away. I believed in my own ability and knew another club would come along, and come along they did, a couple of years later in the shape of Norwich City. They saw me and I signed as an apprentice. Ron Saunders was the manager and he gave me my debut at 18 against a Manchester United team that included Bobby Charlton. I loved Norwich and the fans loved me but as so often happens in football after a change of manager at the club in the shape of John Bond, I found myself, in December 1973, on my way home to Bristol City for £30,000 as part of a young and exciting team being put together by Alan Dicks at Ashton Gate.

"I played in various derbies for City and I know what it meant to the players. You only had to look at Frankie Prince and Gerry Gow kicking lumps out of each other to see that, let alone what it meant to the supporters. Derbies are a special thing, you win and you have the keys to the City so to speak. You loose and you will be in hiding until the next one. Before a Rovers match, myself and the other Bristolians in the side would go around the dressing room telling the other players what the game meant. I would say 'You live here but we come from here, this is our game, if you want to go out with your wives and *girlfriends tonight, win because if you loose, it will be a night in for you.' I am sure the Bristolians in the next dressing room said the same.*

"I *remember the game at Ashton Gate in our promotion year. It was early on in the season and we were lying in sixth place but had come off the back of two away defeats against Hull City and Southampton. Rovers had come off a draw at Cardiff City in the League Cup. Rovers took the lead after three minutes when Alan Warboys smashed a free kick on the edge of the box and it hit Bruce Bannister on the leg which wrong footed Ray Cashley in goal and the ball went in. On the 19th minute Trevor Tainton who was back for City in midfield, played a ball up to me. I went to jump and flicked it on against Stuart Taylor, the Rovers centre-half. As I was about to rise I thought 'that's too high', so I dropped back down but Taylor was still in the air and it went over his head. I just ran on to it and put it past big Jim Eadie in the Rovers goal for my first goal of the season. As Jim came out he caught me with a two-footed tackle catching me just below both knees. I thought both legs were broken so my celebrations were nothing more than a hand in the air to acknowledge the roar of the City crowd. Jim was a big lad and could be very mobile when he wanted to be. I remember he patted me on the head while I was having treatment and he said 'You will be alright'."*

In fact it was Eadie who kept Rovers in it for the rest of the game, pulling off save after save to deny City the win. Although, Rovers nearly snatched it at the end when debutante Tony Pulis lobbed wide of Ray Cashley. The game ended 1-1.

"I *bought Jim a beer in the players lounge after the game and we had a bit of banter about the goal and Jim's barely legal tackle. All of a sudden people were drawn to the window overlooking the car park at Ashton Gate. A mob of City and Rovers so-called fans were fighting each other and going at it hammer and tongs. I'm sad to say it was indicative of the 1970s. It was the height of football hooliganism all over the country and nothing brought it to a head more than a good old local derby. Jim and I were at the window, pints in hand, and we banged on the window. They looked up and saw us. Suddenly they stopped fighting and the City fans started singing 'Cheesley, Cheesley, Cheesley'. Not to be outdone, a cry of 'Eadie, Eadie, Eadie', came up. We waved and went back to our seats. As we did, someone shouted 'They're back fighting again'."*

The 1975 season was to be one of the greatest in City's history. They finished second to Sunderland, securing promotion to Division One. Rovers on the other hand, finished 17th. City opened their season in the big time with a 1-0 win against the mighty Arsenal at Highbury with a team which included Malcolm MacDonald, a £330,000 summer signing from Newcastle United and a fee that was a British record at the time. But on this hot August day, the moment belonged to Bristol City, and Paul Cheesley got the winner. Things were really taking off for Paul. He had already turned down an England under 23 cap choosing instead to play for City against Sunderland, and there were all sorts of rumours of clubs that were interested in offering big money for him. So with his confidence sky high, City played their first home league game midweek against Stoke City. It was to be a night every City fan would remember and Paul would never forget.

"I *just remember going for a ball in the air with Peter Shilton and falling awkwardly. I knew it was serious. I had never known pain like it. Apparently I had ripped my cartilage, tore ligaments and chipped a bone in the knee. Nobody knew the extent of the injury. In fact at first the knee was just iced and after working on my own the knee was the size of a balloon. I even came back a couple of weeks later and played against Birmingham City, it was ridiculous. Operation after operation followed including 36 weeks of rehab but I knew it was not looking good. I trained so hard on my own up and down the Dolman Stand but it still wasn't right. I would have diagnosis after diagnosis, specialist after specialist, and all with a different view on the injury. I knew things weren't looking good. Then as my contract was up for renewal I was summoned to the boardroom and I was told that it was all over for me. At the height of my career, six clubs had come in with bids of £250,000 for me but I had been insured for just £50,000. So I was given my percentage which was £10,000 and given a testimonial against my old club Norwich City. The date was changed twice and when it did go ahead the gate was 4,000."*

What of Paul today?

"I have two kids and I have a grandchild. Home is Whitchurch in Bristol and I run a pub nearby. After leaving football I did various jobs from taxi driver to repping. I do look back on those times with City and I'm privileged to have been part of a great era for the club. I still do bits and pieces for them and it's great to meet up with old players and chat to the fans – after all, they are the important ones."

And the injury?

"Yes it could have been handled better. I should have been seen by a specialist straight away instead of training on it; running up and down the stands with an ice pack on it. I still carry the scars today and I'm on my second knee replacement. I believe life will throw you a problem and you have to believe in yourself to overcome it."

It's that determination and self belief first shown by a 14-year-old Cheesley that made him the player he was and the man he is today: a fighter.

Peter Aitken

What's he doing here?

Gloucester Cup Final

29/04/1974

Bristol City	0-2	Bristol Rovers
		Staniforth 12 mins
		Rudge 23 mins

HT 0-2
Att 15,986

Bristol City: Cashley, Sweeney, Drysdale, Gow, Collier, Merrick, Tainton, Mann, Cheesley, Fear, Gillies, substitute: Ritchie.

Bristol Rovers: Eadie, Jacobs, Parsons, Aitken, Taylor, Prince, Fearnley, Stanton, Warboys, Rudge, Staniforth, substitute: Dobson.

To some Rovers fans Peter Aitken was the ex-player who at one point in his career could've made their dream come true: he could've sent their local rivals into administration and we could possibly have ended up with only one side in Bristol. A fans favourite at Eastville, Peter went to Bristol City where, after two years, he was part of the Ashton eight that ended up saving the club.

"*It's a time in my career which a lot of my Rovers mates give me stick about, and I suppose at the time if I had been a bit more ruthless who knows what would've happened? It was certainly a big challenge for me at the time.*"

And that's something Peter has never shirked on or off the field.

Born in Penarth, South Wales, the young Aitken was spotted by Rovers' legendary South Wales scouting network, playing in the Cardiff league.

"*I signed schoolboy forms for Rovers aged 12 years of age and that's where my love for the club started. I went through the system at Rovers and made my debut at home to Chesterfield on 29/08/1972 in a 2-2 draw. I was 18 and loved every minute of it. I remember getting the shirt before I went out and thinking 'Right Pete this is what you have been working towards for the last 10 years: to be a professional footballer', and I had a good game.*"

It was to be 18 months before Peter sampled his first Bristol derby.

"*The rivalry with City really started at youth team level. We would play City every year and they were* really hard, passionate games and you looked forward to them. I always got the feeling that the club were preparing you for the big first team game against them. It was the same at reserve team level. It was the game you always looked for when the fixtures came out. They were always midweek and under floodlights and that was so special. In those days both managers would field their strongest side, not like today where they put a few kids in and a few trial lists. This was still a big game and it was a game you never wanted to loose.

"I remember my first derby. It was at City in the Gloucester Cup. It was a full house and the atmosphere was electric. The year was 1974 and we went into it after winning promotion to Division Two. City had struggled that year in Division Two so we were full of confidence."

That Rovers confidence showed when after 12 minutes a bad back pass by City's Gerry Sweeney to Gerry Gow was intercepted by Rovers' Frankie Prince. He sent Gordon Fearnley off down the right towards the City goal and his cross somehow came off City goalkeeper Ray Cashley's chest and it fell to Staniforth to blast Rovers 1-0 up. City barely had a shot on goal and it got worse for them. In the 23rd minute, Alan Warboys held up the ball and pushed it to John Rudge who looked up and let fly around 20 yards. His effort flew past Cashley and put Rovers 2-0 up at half-time.

The second half had both teams cancelling each other out, although late on an excellent tackle from Aitken stopped debutante Jimmy Mann breaking through for City. Rovers had the game sewn up and on the 90th minute Stuart Taylor lifted the trophy for the "gas".

"I loved those Gloucester Cup games. The medals were solid gold and there was nothing like beating your rivals and getting to parade a trophy round. When I look back at derby matches they are so special to a city: to win is everything and to loose is just the worst thing for any player or supporter.

"I know there has been a lot of rubbish spoken about merging the clubs but this city can sustain two teams. Both clubs bring so much to the city and we should be proud of them. They mean so much to so many people and I just hope the modern footballer playing in them today realises what they mean to the fans."

Peter's career went from strength to strength at Eastville but there was always a burning desire to test himself to see if he could do it at another club and give himself a challenge.

"I thought long and hard. Changes were happening behind the scenes at the club, not necessarily for the best I thought. I was a senior pro and I just wanted a challenge. I thought it would be good for me. I made my mind up and didn't sign a contract. I thought there was no point if I wanted to go and see if I could play somewhere else. But I think looking back that hurt the manager Terry Cooper. The board obviously thought if we're not playing him, we're not paying him. I remember coming in for training one day. I pulled up in the car park and Terry came over to me and said 'The board have decided to give you seven days notice', and that was it. I went home and thought 'I'm unemployed'."

Peter had played 234 games for Rovers and scored three goals and it wasn't long before Graham Taylor at Watford, along with Howard Kendall at Blackburn Rovers, invited him up.

"I went to both clubs for a week and did well but nothing came of it. Then on my return to Bristol I got a call from Ken Wimshurst at City and he told me Bob Houghton had just joined as manager and wanted me to come over for a week. I must admit I did think 'Oh my god', but I had no money coming in and it was my job, so I went and did well and signed on a free contract in 1980. The move didn't go down well with some of my friends, they said 'Pete, how could you?' But I always used to say 'It's my job, I have to provide for my family and I just want to play football'.

"I made my debut for City away at Shrewsbury Town and we got beat 4-0. Afterwards, Bob Houghton came up to me and said 'Great performance, I still can't believe they let you go', although with the result I thought he was taking the Mick but he meant it. It was strange putting on the red shirt but the lads were great to me, they knew me well and I knew them but I'm sure there were a few thinking 'Christ, what's he doing here?' and at times I thought the same thing. I knew the fans would give me stick and I certainly had my critics. They even booed me in the warm-up in some games, but if I wanted an easy life I wouldn't have gone to Ashton in the first place. I left Rovers to test myself and there was no better test than crossing the city to join their bitter rivals. I know it's not easy for supporters to accept someone who has been a thorn in their team's side, playing for their rivals. I did understand the stick I got and how some of the die hard reds felt. It taught me a lot about myself and my character."

In 1982 Peter's career threw up possibly the biggest challenge of all.

"During my time at City I had picked up that maybe everything wasn't quite right. I had been at Rovers and they were a club without deep pockets but everything was done right. The alarm bells rang for me at City and I didn't feel it was being run well on an admin level. Then one day we were told that these players had to report to the boardroom on Monday morning: Aitken, Merrick, Rodgers, Marshall, Tainton, Garland, Sweeney and Jimmy Mann. I remember Trevor Tainton saying to me 'What do you reckon that's about Pete?', and I said 'I think it's the sack', Trevor laughed but I believed it. I just had a gut feeling about that Monday morning. When we arrived we went into the boardroom and were told that to save the club we had to give up our contracts.

"Obviously people were surprised. I remember the Professional Footballers' Association chairman Gordon Taylor came to the club to find out what was going on. We met at a hotel in Bristol and I will always remember it. He had a safety pin holding the turn-up in his trousers up and I couldn't take my eyes off it. We then left the meeting and unbeknown to us the world and his wife were outside the room. As we left, hundreds of flashes went off as they took pictures. It startled us, particularly Gordon who ushered us back into another room. He said 'My god this is massive'. He arranged to meet the press the next day.

"We met them and Gordon had a new suit on for the press. I think it hit him how big this story was going to be and he obviously wasn't prepared for it. Much was made of the pressure. I think we all knew deep down inside we were going to have to save the club. Looking back on it, being an ex-Rovers player I could've held the club to ransom and held out for more money as all eight had to agree the offer on the table. But that isn't my way. Even though Rovers fans say to me today that I could've let them go under, I have to be honest, it never entered my head.

"We eventually ripped up our contracts and were advised that we had to go and sign on at the job centre as we were technically out of work. The press were waiting for us when we arrived which wasn't a good experience. It was as if they were gloating in our downfall, but that is what sells papers unfortunately."

Pete left City after playing 41 games for the club and within a couple of months he went with Gerry Sweeney to York City where he played 18 games and secured their footballing future by keeping them in Division Four. But when new manager Denis Smith arrived

Pete found himself looking for another club. After a spell in Hong Kong he dropped into non-league football and now finds himself back at his first love, Bristol Rovers, as community officer.

"I love being at the club. They were a club who looked after me from the age of 12 and gave me a living and allowed me to see the world. I have a good relationship with both City and Rovers fans and I feel privileged to have played for both clubs. I would give anything to be able to put the boots back on and play in a derby game again. They were so special."

Keith Fear

Give it to Keith

League Division Two

28/12/1974

Bristol Rovers	**1-4**	**Bristol City**
Fearnley 26 mins		Fear 58, 90mins
		Mann 72 mins
		Tainton 77 mins

HT 1-0
Att 20,933

Bristol Rovers: Sheppard, Bater, Parsons, Aitken, Taylor, Prince, Fearnley, Coombes, Warboys, Staniforth, Britten, substitute: Jones.

Bristol City: Cashley, Sweeney, Drysdale, Mann, Collier, Merrick, Tainton, Ritchie, Fear, Cheesley, Durrell, substitute: Griffin.

Whenever the 70s are mentioned, I am brought back to memories of riding my chopper bike around Bristol, dancing to Slade at school discos, and playing football in the playground of St. Bernadette's primary school pretending to be one man: not Best, Bowles, Hudson or Currie but Bristol's own entertainer, Keith Fear. Regarded by many as the most skilful and gifted player City had produced in that era, Fear could change a match with one moment of magic and mesmerise every watching schoolboy.

Born in Bristol in 1952, Fear was a prolific goalscorer for his school, Connaught Road, in Knowle and it was his performances at this early age that led to a posse of clubs, including the two from Bristol, battling for the youngster's signature.

"I signed as a schoolboy for City at 13 and went on to represent England twice at under 16 level against Wales and Scotland. Then at 17 I joined the pro ranks at City. I started playing derby matches right from then. We would play Rovers at youth level, combination and the football league, not to mention the Gloucester Cup, a fixture that sadly is no more and a fixture we as players all loved. After all, you could beat your local rivals, get a Cup to parade round and a winner's medal, with bragging rites booked for a whole year. The derby games at that time were great because the majority of players were local or from surrounding areas and I think that made it very special for us.

"The league game in 1974 at Eastville sticks in my mind. The weather was awful with the wind and rain gusting about 70mph from the Tote End towards the Muller Road End and I don't think I have played in a game where the outcome of the game was so dependent on the toss.

"It was Rovers captain Stuart Taylor who won the toss and elected, some say wrongly, to kick with the wind in the first half, but as Taylor pointed out later: 'We always kick towards the Tote End second half'. Alan Dicks said to us before kick-off that hopefully they will kick with the wind first half and we can see how they cope and adjust our game to suit. If we could contain them first half we could have a right go second half. Our captain Geoff Merrick told the defence that to cope with the wind we would play offside whenever we could, so it's safe to say we did have a game plan."

And that game plan worked until the 26th minute when a shot from Rovers' Britten was parried by City's keeper Ray Cashley out to Gordon Fearnley and with the City defence in disarray and screaming for offside, Fearnley put the gas 1-0 up (in fact after the game referee Gordon Hill admitted two Rovers players were in an offside position).

"We went in 1-0 down at half-time and we were buzzing. We had contained them and couldn't wait for the second half. Our coach Ken Wimshurst said we could get five or six in the second half, but I would have been happy with any old win."

Bristol City made the most of the second half wind and started to put pressure on Rovers keeper Dick Sheppard, who was back in the first team for the first time in two years after an injury to Rovers' first choice keeper Jim Eadie in the previous game at Aston Villa. To say Dick wasn't having the best of days was an understatement. He was struggling with his kicking due to the wind and on the 57th minute things got worse for the Rovers keeper. A corner from City's Durrell was sliced by Geoff Merrick and Fear nipped in to put City level. On the 72nd minute Sheppard was caught napping when Jimmy Mann cut inside Lindsay Parsons and drove a shot that beat Sheppard on the near post.

"I knew then Rovers wouldn't score and for us it was a matter of how many we would get."

City went further ahead five minutes later when Trevor Tainton hit home a cracking 18 yard shot that left Sheppard stranded.

"I didn't really want the game to end as I knew we could get more and on the 90th minute I got my second. I just saw the ball coming from Ray Cashley's kick and I didn't think anyone would get to it. It bounced 30 yards from the goal so I just turned, ran, and hit it. I knew when it left my foot it was going in."

The game ended 4-1 to City. They finished fifth that season and Rovers were 19th. Unfortunately for Dick Sheppard it was his last game for Rovers, and many fans feel it was the fractured skull he sustained at Tranmere a year earlier that stopped this Rovers great from being at his best that windswept day. Keith was an integral part of a very good side that Alan Dicks had put together, culminating in promotion to the First Division in 1976.

"We were team mates and friends on and off the field. We had played together a long time and knew each other's strengths and weaknesses. Many a time they would shout 'Give it to Keith', mainly so I would keep the ball while we re-grouped or had a breather and to be fair they knew I was never going to track back and defend very often much to the dismay of manager Alan Dicks."

In 1977, after falling out with Dicks, Keith left for Plymouth Argyle where he stayed for two seasons, then moved to Chester City.

"Although me and Alan Dicks didn't see eye to eye regarding my best position, I have to say he was the best manager City ever had. He did what nobody has done and brought top flight football to Bristol. I worked with Malcolm Allison at Plymouth then Alan Oakes at Chester City and I learnt from them all but City was my home and where I played my best football. I dropped into non-league with Bangor City but my knees were in a bad state by then. I still had league clubs asking me to play for them however, I could play but not train.

"I now work for a fruit and vegetable wholesaler in Bristol and I have done it for over 20 years. It's a job I love and I still get a buzz out of selling but the buzz is nothing compared to the buzz of pulling on the red shirt. People still recognise me today and ask for autographs which is great and that's both City and Rovers fans."

Keith finished at Bristol City with around 35 goals from 170 games. Some would say that's not a great return from someone so talented but for anyone who saw Keith play it was good enough for us.

Tony Pulis

It was then I realised what it meant to Bristol

League Division Two

30/08/1975

Bristol City	**1-1**	**Bristol Rovers**
Cheesley 19 mins		Bannister 3 mins

HT 1-1
Att 17,918

Bristol City: Cashley, Sweeney, Drysdale, Gow, Collier, Merrick, Tainton, Ritchie, Mann, Cheesley, Brolly, substitute: Gillies.

Bristol Rovers: Eadie, Smith, Williams, Aitken, Taylor, Prince, Stephens, Pulis, Warboys, Bannister, Evans, substitute: Fearnley.

The atmosphere at a Bristol derby can be an intimidating experience for many a seasonal professional let alone someone making their debut, but that's what happened to a 17-year-old Tony Pulis. When he took the field that hot summer's afternoon I'm sure he could only dream that it would become the start of a career that would take him to the very top in management and it was not to be the first time he had experienced a hostile Ashton Gate.

"I was born in Newport, South Wales and was spotted as a schoolboy by Rovers' legendary scouting network in Wales at that time. People like Stan Montgomery, Bill Dodgin and Bobby Campbell were tremendous people to be around when learning your trade as a player. They instilled good habits in all us lads and Rovers were a great club to be part of.

"I remember my debut vividly. Don Megson, our boss, told me I was playing on the Thursday and I was over the moon to be playing but didn't really think about it being the derby match. Then as the game got nearer, the local press featured me and so did the TV but I wasn't particularly nervous. We drove into Ashton Gate on the afternoon of the match and as I passed the old Open End there was a sea of blue and white. The noise from the ground was unbelievable and it was then I realised what it meant to Bristol, and to be honest the nerves kicked in. We had good old pros who were more than willing to look after a youngster from the Valley – Frankie Prince being one of them. He told me I would be OK and to enjoy it."

Rovers scored first through Bruce Bannister and City replied in the 19th minute with Paul Cheesley.

"I had a good game and I think we both punched each other out in the second half. I found the game really quick and a lot more physical than my combination and reserve games."

Then with 14 minutes to go City's suspect offside trap let Pulis through on goal with Ray Cashley to beat.

"I can't really remember much about it but I remember waiting for the linesman to call offside but it didn't happen, so I carried on and tried to lob it but it went wide. When the game ended I was just relieved to have had a good game and the lads were brilliant to me."

Tony went on to play for Rovers regularly but after a bad injury at 21 he obtained his FA coaching badge and his UEFA B license, becoming one of the youngest professional players ever to obtain the qualification. In 1981, under David Williams, Tony became player-coach with Rovers but left the club in 1984 to go to Newport County. Spells at Gillingham and Bournemouth followed and it was at Bournemouth that Tony got his first taste of the manager hot-seat after Harry Redknapp left for West Ham. The Bournemouth board turned to Tony and his management career started. After two years at Bournemouth and a spell at Gillingham, the Welshman found himself appointed manager of Bristol City in 1999.

"I had no qualms about taking the City job and I knew I might get some stick due to my Rovers connection. They were a really big club with huge potential and I wasn't the sort of person to duck a challenge.

"To say my time at City was eventful is an understatement. I remember one training session it was pouring with rain and I was working the first team squad with my assistant Lindsay Parsons, another ex-Rovers star, and things were going well with the crowd at the time. Lindsay borrowed the red cap I always wore and Tony Fawthrop, the chief scout, appears and says we need to go to the ground immediately. So we finish the session and go. We enter the boardroom and are greeted by Stephen Lansdown and two members of the CID from Avon and Somerset constabulary. They then told me they had received death threats about me and they had to take them seriously as they had mentioned my home address; they said they are watching me and see me about always wearing a red baseball cap. At that precise moment Lindsay took my hat off his head and put it back on my head. We all fell about laughing but obviously we had to take it seriously. I wasn't too bothered by a few nutters who told the police what they wanted to do to me. I always thought if you were serious you wouldn't tell the police anyway.

"I can also remember winning my first home game and as I walked off at Ashton Gate I was booed by a section of the crowd. Lindsay Parsons looked at me and said 'You're not gonna get anything here Tony' and I suppose it was a tough old job, but I have to say there are some great people at City. Steve Lansdown and John Laycock were wonderful to me and to be honest the supporters are passionate and there's nothing wrong with that. It was just one of those things at the time. It just didn't work out for both of us, but I honestly have to say I would love to see them or Rovers in the top flight. The people of Bristol deserve that."

Tony left City in January 2000 to join Portsmouth. He had been in charge of City for 33 games: he won 10, lost 9 and drew 14. After Portsmouth and Plymouth, Stoke beckoned and it is at Stoke where he now plies his trade pitting his wits against the very best in the Premier League.

"I *always look for Rovers scores and they will always be my club. I was extremely fortunate to be with a club like* Rovers. *They looked after us and were a very homely club. I feel privileged to have played with the blue half of the city and to have managed the red half, and of my debut I think I'm lucky to have made it in a local derby. The atmosphere that day certainly prepared me for the rest of my career."*

Martin Hirst

Before I knew it, I was engulfed by team mates

FA Cup Second Round

10/12/1983

Bristol Rovers	**1-2**	**Bristol City**
Stephens 50 mins		*Ritchie 78 mins*
		Hirst 89 mins

HT 0-0
Att 14,396

Bristol Rovers: Kite, Slatter, B. Williams, Bater, Parkin, McCaffery, Holloway, G. Williams, Stephens, Randall, Barrett, substitute: White.

Bristol City: Shaw, Stevens, G. Williams, Halliday, Phillipston-Masters, Stroud, Pritchard, Ritchie, Hirst, Riley, Crawford, substitute: Cooper.

Martin Hirst's appearance in this book, owes as much to his unconventional background as to his winning goal at this December derby. An English schoolboy international who went to America to coach, on his return he went to Bristol University to study geography where he played for the university football team whilst also donning the colours of Bath City.

"I was in my early twenties and although I had thoughts of becoming a P.E. teacher and getting my degree, I decided to write to various clubs to try and see if I could make it as a player. City gave me an outing for the reserves in a Western league game against Ottery St. Mary. I don't remember the result but I know I did OK, and I got a part-time contract which suited me fine.

"I made my debut at home to Chesterfield in a 2-0 win. The Cup game will always be with me. In the build-up we were given no chance by the media. We were lying seventh in Division Four and Rovers were second in Division Three and had beaten us in the last five meetings. On the Friday before the game, Terry Cooper and Clive Middlemass unveiled their secret plan. They moved right-winger Howard Pritchard to partner Glyn Riley upfront, and pushed me to the right side of midfield. I'm sure the tactic unsettled Rovers' back four.

"When we arrived at Eastville, I had never experienced anything remotely like the atmosphere of a big Bristol derby and it was only my fourth appearance for the club. The noise when we took the field was enough to give anyone pre-match nerves, but the strange thing was that as soon as the game kicked off I forgot all about it. Because of the media hype before, we felt like we had nothing to loose, and it showed *in our football throughout the 90 minutes.*

"After playing slightly better in the first half we fell behind to a superb Archie Stephens header after the interval, but it only served to make us push more men forward and put pressure on their defenders. Manager Terry Cooper came on as substitute (it was the 47th Cup tie of his career) and had his customary effect of calming us down. We created one or two chances and it was no surprise when Tom Ritchie shot a superbly taken equaliser after a good build-up on the right. We were more than happy with a replay and started to think in terms of avoiding any mistakes but with the gaffer on the field controlling things there was always a chance we would set up another goal scoring opportunity."

So it proved with just a couple of minutes left Neil Slatter attempted to let through a ball from Terry Cooper run out of play but Glyn Riley made an excellent interception and drew keeper Phil Kite out of position.

"Glyn looked like he was going to shoot but at the last moment he squared the ball to me on the six yard line. I don't know how I managed to get there because I was exhausted but I do remember mis-hitting my shot and seeing the ball creep over the line. Before I knew it, I was engulfed by team mates and heard the manager calling me a lucky so and so for scoring such a muffed effort. I was on cloud nine and managed to give the ball away a few times in the short time remaining. Fortunately Rovers failed to take advantage and when the final whistle went I was acclaimed the hero.

"I recall trying to give a radio interview on the touchline as we left the field, but I was so out of breath that I don't think anyone could have understood what I said. There was champagne in the dressing room and tremendous scenes of celebration, then it was back to Ashton Gate where the drinks were on the chairman, and players had a night to remember. I remember thinking that night that I wanted to concentrate on becoming a regular in the first team."

Bristol City were knocked out in the third round by a very good First Division Notts County side 2-0 at Ashton Gate, after drawing the first leg at Meadow Lane 1-1. Martin went on to become an important part of the promotion winning team, but at his own admission he found the step up very difficult, and in September 1985 he went on loan to Torquay United and then was transferred to Weymouth.

"After Weymouth I played for various non-league sides: Chesham United, St. Albans and Wealston. I got my geography degree and now I work for a travel company in St. Albans. I will never forget that day. It was the pinnacle of my career, and although things didn't work out long term at Bristol City I will always have a soft spot for them."

Martin Hirst came into the FA Cup tie a relative unknown even with some of the City fans, but it's safe to say he left that Eastville pitch a hero, at least with the red half of the city.

Paul Randall

Punky scores again

FA Cup Second Round

08/12/1984

Bristol City	**1-3**	**Bristol Rovers**
Halliday 4 mins		O'Connor 8 mins
		Randall 18, 42 mins

HT 1-3
Att 19,367

Bristol City: Hooper, Llewellyn, Curle, Phillipston-Masters, Halliday, Pritchard, Stroud, Hirst, Walsh, Hutchinson, Riley, substitute: Ritchie.

Bristol Rovers: Cashley, Slatter, Parkin, McCaffery, Bater, Holloway, D. Williams, B. Williams, O'Connor, Stephens, Randall, substitute: G. Williams.

With the "Smash and Grab" era of Warboys and Bannister gone who would've thought the next Tote End hero would've been a supermarket worker from Glastonbury, Paul "Punky" Randall. The slightly built, devastatingly quick striker was an instant hit with the Eastville crowd from day one and that mutual respect continues to this day.

"As a kid I had trials at Bristol Rovers, Bristol City, Cardiff City and Manchester City. I was encouraged to go to Rovers by ex-player George Petherbridge who lived near me. I played a few games for the youth team and reserves and I scored a few goals but missed out on an apprenticeship and nothing really happened with the other clubs. I went back to playing local football with Glastonbury and Frome and scoring goals.

"Job wise I was at the supermarket but I knew I would at some point get my chance. Frome then had a pre-season friendly against Rovers' reserves on a Tuesday night and we beat them 2-0 and I had a great game.

"Colin Dobson, Rovers' assistant manager, came up to me afterwards and said 'I have spoken to the Rovers manager Don Megson about you and here's a contract. If you want it, see you at Eastville on Monday.'

"I was 19. I went into the supermarket the next day and quit my job, even though the contract at Rovers was less money."

Paul played in various matches for the reserves including a 6-0 win against Trowbridge in which he scored four.

Wayne Powell was injured for the first team in a league Cup game away at Walsall and Paul was thrown into the opening match of the 1977 season away at Cardiff City. Paul had a dream start scoring Rovers' goal in a 1-1 draw; he then went on to score in Rovers' opening home game to Notts County, a game that ended 2-2. He was an instant hit with the Tote End faithful, netting four goals in his first five games. The Ninian Park debut not only produced Paul's first goal but it was where the nickname "Punky" was born.

"I was sat in the dressing room thinking about the game and to be honest I was miles away. The radio was on in the corner and I think a Clash or Sex Pistols song came on and I just sang a couple of words. In the corner a few older pros were playing cards and I think Phil Bater or Peter Aitken looked up and shouted 'Oi, look at Punky over there!', and it stuck ever since. Although when I had my perm in the 80s some of the Rovers faithful called me 'Shirley'."

That debut season saw Paul score 20 goals. It also included a Cup run for Rovers that saw them knock out First Division Southampton 2-0 with Paul getting both goals. The win thrust the former supermarket worker into the national spotlight and there were endless pictures of Paul with the obligatory shopping trolley glaring out from various tabloid back pages. It wasn't long before an offer from a bigger club came Rovers' way and in December 1978 Paul joined Stoke City for £180,000. He had scored 33 goals in 49 games for Rovers.

"It was all done quickly. I met Alan Durban, the Stoke manager, and hours later I had signed and was a Stoke player. I went because I wanted to play at a higher level and at the end of that season I helped Stoke win promotion to the First Division."

Over the next few years Paul was in and out of the Stoke side and it wasn't long before Terry Cooper, the then Rovers manager, brought him back to Rovers although a late interest from Bristol City nearly scrapped the deal.

"I was at the Crest Hotel at Hambrook and I had just agreed to come back to Rovers after talks with Terry Cooper when I had a call at reception. I went down and it was Bobby Houghton, the then City manager, asking if I would be interested in coming to Ashton Gate. I said 'No, I have agreed to go to Rovers' and I thought if I did go I would get lynched by both sets of supporters."

So in January 1981 Bristol Rovers paid Stoke £55,000 for Paul's signature, and it was during this second spell at the club he played in his favourite derby.

"It was an FA Cup second round tie at Ashton Gate in 1984, a month before they had beaten us 3-0 in the league and to be honest they murdered us and I was subbed. So when we huddled around the radio after training at Hambrook to listen to the Cup draw and away at Bristol City came out, we weren't filled with a great deal of confidence."

It was a packed, intimidating Ashton Gate that greeted the Rovers team that December afternoon and it was to get worse after five minutes when Rovers gave away a free kick outside the box thinking City's Alan Walsh was going to hit his trademark thunderbolt but instead he produced a lovely chip for Bruce Halliday to head past Cashley.

"I thought, here we go again, what a start, this is going to be a long afternoon."

But four minutes later, an Ian Holloway cross was met by possibly the smallest player in the team, Mark O'Connor, and Rovers were level. The game had exploded into life and on 15 minutes Rovers suffered a setback when a bad challenge from Alan Walsh (one he later apologised for) left Rovers full-back Neil Slatter having to go off with a badly gashed leg, so Rovers brought on midfielder Geraint Williams to play as a makeshift right-back. Randall struck in the 18th minute when a ball from player-manager David Williams sent Randall off on a run. City's Keith Curle tried to stay with him but was outpaced by Randall. The Rovers striker put the ball past Hooper in the City goal, in front of the East End.

"As I put the ball away I remember turning to celebrate and getting terrible stick from the City fans."

Then just before half-time Holloway, who was tremendous, played a ball into Randall in the box and as City pleaded for offside Paul put Rovers 3-1 up.

"We went in at half-time with such confidence. We didn't want the half to end."

The second half was never going to live up to the first 45 minutes and it seemed both teams had punched themselves out. The chances for both teams were few and far between, and on 90 minutes the referee blew for a Rovers win.

"I remember after the game I met up with my dad and some friends from Glastonbury who had come to the game and we went upstairs to the 51 Club at Ashton Gate. It was full of gas heads singing '1-0 down 3-1 up we knocked City out the Cup!'. The atmosphere was great. That night after a few drinks on the way home, I got back to my mum and dad's in Glastonbury and my younger sister Gail had gone out on a first date with a lad who was a City fan and he refused to come in the house."

Rovers drew Ipswich in the third round and went out 2-1 at home with Ian Holloway getting the Rovers goal. Then in 1986 Paul left Rovers and as it turned out, league football. He was 28 and had scored 105 goals in over 270 matches.

"Bobby Gould was manager and he didn't really rate me. I went to Yeovil and to be honest I was sure a league club would come in. There was interest from Cardiff City but nothing happened."

Paul went on to play for Bath City, Frome and Weymouth and he finished full circle playing for Glastonbury. He retired from football aged 47.

"I loved my time at Rovers and I love the fans. Whenever I go back they always give me a good reception and it means a lot to me. Today I work in a pharmacy as a dispenser which is quite ironic given the state of my knees but I have done it for about 15 years and love it. I am married and have two great kids; both sport minded – Mark plays football and Kelly plays netball – both County standard. I get a real kick out of seeing them play and they love it when people stop me and say 'Didn't you used to be Punky Randall?'."

Alan Walsh

The moment it left my head I knew it was in

League Division Three

12/09/1987

Bristol City	3-3	Bristol Rovers
Walsh 38 mins		*Jones 9 mins*
Fitzpatrick 65 mins		*Reece 56 mins*
Moyes 73 mins		*Holloway 83 mins*

HT 1-1
Att 14,746

Bristol City: Waugh, Llewellyn, Moyes, Newman, Bromage, Marshall, Fitzpatrick, Galliers, Walsh, Jordan, Neville, substitutes: Caldwell, Tanner.

Bristol Rovers: Carter, Alexander, Jones, Twentyman, Tanner, Holloway, Hibbitt, Reece, Purnell, Penrice, White, substitutes: Turner, Carr.

Alan Walsh was the Bristol City jewel that the top clubs never discovered. How this power house of a striker from the footballing hot bed of the north east never played top flight football the fans at Ashton Gate will never know. Born in Hartlepool, the young Alan was working full time for a brick company and playing local football on the weekends.

"When I was younger I had clubs look at me but nothing came of it but then I got a call from Middlesbrough who wanted me to go for a month's trial. I spoke to my employers who were great and said go for it but whatever happens we want you to come back and finish your apprenticeship so I agreed and off I went. The month went well and they signed me and I started playing regularly for the reserves and made three substitute appearances for the first team and I was really happy. Then out of the blue, manager John Neal told me they had accepted an offer from Darlington who at the time were in the Fourth Division. I was about 22 years old and had a real chance of first team football so I grabbed it."

And grab it he did. Over the course of six years at the club Walsh scored 87 goals in 251 games and became a Darlington legend and the club's record scorer. So you would think offer after offer would flood in and a big money move would be on the cards, but not for Walsh.

"The year before I came to City we were playing them at Ashton Gate and Terry Cooper was manager and I knew Terry from when he was at Boro. As we entered the players entrance I went to turn right to the away team's dressing room but a voice called out 'Walshie' and it was Terry. He called me into his

office and asked me to come to the club but he told me he couldn't pay any more than £20,000 for me. I said I would think about it."

So Bristol City made their offer of £18,000 and it fell very short of Darlington's £85,000 valuation for their record goalscorer and so the fee was settled by a tribunal and Alan Walsh joined Bristol City in 1984 for the sum of £18,000. That must be the best £18,000 ever spent by the club to this day. As soon as Alan pulled on the red shirt it was plain to see that the robins had got a gem. He made his debut at home to Wigan and never looked back.

"Coming from the north east I knew all about derbies with Newcastle and Sunderland and to a lesser extent Darlington and Hartlepool but I never dreamed what a Bristol one would be like, particularly because it was two teams one city and I had never experienced that before.

"It's not until you have experienced it that you really appreciate it. I couldn't believe the passion of the fans. It was a real eye opener for me and I loved it. My first one was at Ashton Gate in a league match around 1984. We won 3-0 and we were easily the better side. I think Glyn Riley got two that day but yes it was a great game to be part of. The game I remember most though was in September 1987 again at Ashton Gate."

The 1987 derby at Ashton Gate was certainly a scintillating affair. The last couple of games between the two sides had been dour 1-0 or 0-0 games and this match in front of over 14,000 broke the mould. All the passion and drama that had eluded the last couple of matches had returned.

Rovers opened the scoring on nine minutes when Keith Waugh gave away a free kick for handling outside his goal. The resulting free kick taken by Bristol Rovers' Vaughan Jones, crashed into the net leaving Waugh nowhere. Rovers deserved their lead as they had gone close with Devon White and Phil Purnell early on. Referee Keren Barrett certainly had to take control as Andy Llewellyn found his name in the book after chopping down Rovers' Purnell and Steve Neville almost became the second City player in the book after an altercation with Ian Alexander. City's equaliser came on 38 minutes when Gary Marshall left Rovers' Nicky Tanner standing and his right cross was met perfectly by Alan who headed home. Walsh almost made it 2-1 minutes later when a trademark bullet of a free kick was saved by Tim Carter in the Rovers goal. City were on the up. Rovers' frustration boiled over and both Geoff Twentyman and Kenny Hibbitt found themselves booked just before half-time.

"We didn't want half-time to come as we were playing really well. We were the better side and knew we had goals in us. As for my goal, the moment it left my head I knew it was in."

Rovers came out in the second half on the attack and on 56 minutes Andy Reece found space just outside the box and hit a sweet shot to beat Waugh in the top corner. City thought they had got level minutes later when Joe Jordan found the net only to be denied by the linesman's flag. But level they got on 65 minutes when Rovers' keeper Tim Carter rashly ran out to meet a Russell Bromage cross and was beaten to it by Paul Fitzpatrick whose header found an unguarded net and put City level. Rovers then pushed on and Waugh produced the save of the game to stop a point blank header from Gary Penrice. Rovers rued the chance minutes later when Jordan headed down a Bromage free kick and

City's David Moyes buried the ball home and set the Ashton Gate fans into raptures. City almost put the game out of sight of Rovers when Neville put the ball in the Rovers net but was denied by another offside decision. Despite this, Rovers, true to form, never gave up and were rewarded seven minutes from time when Bromage's clearance found Ian Holloway who jinked his way into the City penalty area before curling a low shot in off the post to finish the game 3-3.

"We were gutted at the end and we felt like we had lost but credit to them they never gave up and it was a great match to be part of. It was a real advert for Bristol football and I will always remember it."

Alan went on to play over 200 games for City and scored 77 goals and in 1989 he had an offer to go to Turkey to play for Besiktas who, at the time, were managed by former Coventry manager Gordon Milne.

"My contract was up and the offer was too good to turn down. I had a wife and kids and although it was hard leaving City I went for it."

Alan played for two seasons winning the league title twice and the Turkish Cup, also playing in Europe, but there was always a strong desire to come home as Turkey was never going to be a long term thing for him and his family.

"I loved it in Turkey but came back and I came to City where Jimmy Lumsden was manager and he said, 'Let us have a look at you and talk about signing you'. So I played in a few reserve games but nothing happened and I ended up leaving which was really sad because I would've loved to have got a contract and been able to pull that red shirt on again but it was not to be. It was 1991 and I ended up having more clubs in that season than I had had in my whole career. I was at Walsall, Huddersfield, Shrewsbury and Cardiff, and I also played over in Ireland. I ended up just going from club to club playing anywhere they needed a player and after a while I thought 'This has got to stop'."

Alan then dropped into non-league football playing for Clevedon Town and also Taunton where he played at Wembley against Diss Town in the FA trophy final, and it was at Taunton he received a call from his home town club Hartlepool.

"They called me and offered me a contract. I thought it was a joke at first and I told them I hadn't played pro for 18 months but they were keen so I went up and signed a year's contract. It was a dream come true to play for my old home town club and finished my career off perfectly especially when I scored on my debut against Gillingham: it was my 200th career goal. After my year was up at Hartlepool a new management team came to the club and what with my age I found myself out of their plans."

Alan had never moved out of the Bristol area and was offered a job at Bristol Rovers as the community officer.

"I loved the job at Rovers and they were brilliant to me. The supporters were great and would give me a bit of stick but only in fun. I loved still being involved in the game. I was at Rovers for four years then was offered a job with Bristol City's Academy which I could not turn down and Rovers knew that and understood. So I went back to Ashton Gate and felt I had come home and now I'm development coach and love working with the youngsters and the first team. Gary Johnson is doing a great job at the club and it's a privilege to be part of it."

Geoff Twentyman

If it had been a boxing bout they would've stopped it

League Division Three

01/01/1987

Bristol City	0-1	Bristol Rovers
		Smart 87 mins

HT 0-0
Att 17,122

Bristol City: Waugh, Newman, MacPhail, Moyes, Williams, Marshall, Fitzpatrick, Curle, Walsh, Riley, Neville, substitute: Hutchinson.

Bristol Rovers: Carter, Jones, Twentyman, Carr, Scales, Smart, Tanner, Weston, Dryden, Mehew, Morgan, substitute: Micallef.

When defender Geoff Twentyman arrived at Bristol Rovers in 1986, off the pitch would prove to be one of the most difficult times for the club, yet on it, the likeable Scouser would go on to be part of a Rovers team that will forever be in the history of the "gas".

There was no better grounding for the young Twentyman: Geoff's father, Geoff senior, had been a Liverpool player in the fifties and went on to be chief scout under the great Bill Shankly, Bob Paisley and Kenny Dalglish and it was in the Liverpool reserves that young Geoff learnt his trade.

"I was at Anfield as a youngster studying A levels and it was quite surreal really as I would be at school in the day then in the evening I would be at Anfield with some of the biggest names in the late seventies at a time when the club appeared to be invincible in Britain and across Europe. To be honest I was never going to make the grade and I think I realised that. I remember going into Bob Paisley's office to find out about whether I was to be kept on and there is a bit of a story about him. People believed that he wore his slippers in his office – I think they thought of him as a sort of favourite granddad type figure. As I said, I had gone in to see him and he was great to me at the time. I had got a place at Chester college to be a P.E. teacher and he basically told me he thought I would be a better P.E. teacher than a footballer. We shook hands and as I looked down he was wearing slippers."

Geoff left the reds and went into non-league football gaining a growing reputation at Chorley Town in the northern league. He was then snapped up by former Everton manager, Gordon Lee, at Preston North End.

"I played at Preston for three years and it was the most unstable club I had ever seen. We had six managers in three seasons; we had relegation and applied for re-election; it was a nightmare. The chairman decided to start afresh and let all the players whose contract had expired leave the club. There were six, and one of them was me. I was the only one to get a club which was due to Rovers manager Bobby Gould meeting Brian Kidd on holiday. Kidd had been manager at Preston and Bobby told him he was after an experienced defender for not much money and Brian said 'Geoff Twentyman will do the job for you'. So Bobby rang me. I have to say I wasn't inundated with offers and on the previous occasions I had played in Bristol the place had looked nice so I thought 'Yes, I will like it down there', not knowing I would stay. So I agreed to come. I remember a guy in my local who was a bit of an anorak telling me 'Oh yes, Bristol Rovers, they're playing at Twerton Park in Bath.'

I said 'No, I don't think so', surely Bobby would've said something?

Anyway, I phoned him and he said 'Yes, I forgot to mention that, but Twerton is one of the best non-league grounds.'

I thought 'This is going to be interesting'."

And interesting it was with Rovers building on that,'through adversity' mentality, creating a team spirit that would see them take the Third Division title four years later under Gerry Francis.

"The Bristol derby I remember most was the first I played in: it was New Year's Day 1987 at Ashton Gate and an 11.30 kick-off. When the fixtures came out, the first game I looked for was City at Ashton Gate. No disrespect to Twerton but Ashton was a real football ground and I used to thrive on the occasion. I never got nervous and I think this went back to my Liverpool days. I used to look at it that being a scouser and playing for Liverpool reserves at Anfield, Old Trafford, Maine Road and even Wembley with Rovers in later years, nothing would've been more nerve racking than being in that first team at Anfield, so consequently I never got nervous playing any other game no matter how big.

"I was brought up on the Liverpool derby: two teams from one city. I had played for Preston against Burnley which was called a derby but I didn't see it that way and that day walking out at Ashton Gate fulfilled an ambition to play in a big derby and I never forgot it. As a player, I think you carry a certain responsibility for the fans. In a derby you don't dislike the other team or their fans but I think as a player you have to be acutely aware that the fans who follow your club have to go to work Monday and it's in your power to make it as easy for them as possible.

"The atmosphere that day was unbelievable. There was chaos at Ashton Gate with 5,000 fans queuing outside to get in as six turnstile operatives did not turn up and it had to be managed by admin staff in the end. A lot of the fans didn't get into the ground until 20 minutes after kick-off and for a lot of them the day didn't get any better."

The game kicked off with Ashton packed to the rafters and it was City who took control testing Tim Carter in the Rovers goal on every available opportunity. But then on the half hour, Carter collided with City's Steve Neville and the Rovers keeper had to go off for stitches to a head wound.

David Mehew went in goal for Rovers and survived without too many alarms, even saving a point blank range shot from City's Alan Walsh until Carter was fit to resume. It was then that there was a growing feeling that it was to be Rovers' day. The second half carried on with the City onslaught. Carter made saves from Walsh, Neville and Fitzpatrick, crashing a ball against the woodwork on the 60th minute. Rovers' willing youngsters found themselves pinned in their own half, unable to get out. On the 75th minute, Neville broke free to score but pushed the ball wide of Carter. The groans from the red half of the city reverberated around the ground. With three minutes remaining Rovers were awarded a free kick in their own half.

"I used to take the free kicks because I could hit them a long way, anyway in those days you could pass back to the keeper to kill the ball and to be honest, with the pressure we had been under, I just wanted to hit it down field. So I stuck it right in the City box. Trevor Morgan went up in the air with City's David Moyes and Moyes won the header. The ball came out to the 'd' on the edge of the box where Gary Smart, who incidentally was a part-time footballer for us and worked full time in the laundry at Frenchay hospital, hit it on the volley and Keith Welch had no chance. It flew into the net and won us the match 1-0. It was absolute daylight robbery! People have been in Horfield prison for less. How we ever won that match I will never know. If it had been a boxing bout they would've stopped it after 20 minutes. Our keeper, the late Tim Carter, was magnificent. We had one chance and took it and that's what wins games. There is nothing better on derby day than shaking hands with your opposite number or the player you're marking and looking him in the eye and saying 'unlucky'. Consequently, there's nothing worse when you've lost. I remember after the game we all had a singsong and a few drinks in the bath. I'm also reminded that in the build-up to the game our manager told us 'If you win against the City lads a local businessman has promised you all brown envelopes with a few quid in for you'. This was typical Bobby psychology and not a hint of a brown envelope in sight."

Geoff went on to be an integral part of a very successful Rovers team under Gerry Francis winning the Third Division and appearing at Wembley in the freight Rover final. When Gerry left for QPR there was talk of Geoff being his natural successor as he had the respect of the players and the fans.

"I wanted the job and made no secret of it to the board. I applied but heard nothing. They then appointed Martin Dobson and then a few weeks after Martin got the job I got a letter saying 'Thanks for your interest in the job but the vacancy has been filled'. It was a bizarre situation. I think when I look back, the time was right for me and I would've loved a crack at it but it wasn't to be."

Geoff had played 252 games for Rovers and scored six goals.

"I always had an eye on what to do when I finished in the game and I was always interested in media. I went on a course at the University of the West of England and learnt how to do bits and pieces with radio and got a qualification which got me in the BBC. I was working in local radio for three years when I then got a call from my old mate Ian Holloway. I was in the BBC newsroom and he told me he was being lined up for the Rovers job and would I be his assistant as he could trust me as we had always been friends. So I accepted, but after a year it didn't quite work out and I'm glad to say our friendship never suffered and fortunately for me I was able to come back to the BBC where I've been ever since."

Geoff is now a successful presenter on BBC Radio Bristol where he hosts the popular Friday phone-in show which gives Rovers and City fans a chance to vent their feelings about their club. He has overcome that difficult hurdle of being respected by both sets of fans, mainly due to his impartiality and vast knowledge of the game. Geoff was obviously given a good grounding at Liverpool in his early days which has helped him in his later career. I just hope he isn't wearing slippers when he's on air.

Rob Newman

Mr 100%

League Division Three

25/03/1989

Bristol Rovers	**1-1**	**Bristol City**
Penrice 26 mins		Walsh 24 mins

HT 1-1
Att 8,679

Bristol Rovers: Martyn, Alexander, Twentyman, Yates, Reece, Jones, Holloway, Bailey, McClean, Penrice, Purnell, substitute: White.

Bristol City: Waugh, Honor, Bailey, Humphries, Pender, Newman, Galliers, McClaren, Taylor, Walsh, Turner, substitute: Mardon.

Rob Newman could and would play anywhere. He was Bristol City's Mr dependable and to the fans he was Mr 100%.

During an 11-year period in which he amassed around 500 games for the club, Rob must have played in every position bar goalkeeper and I'm sure that was only because he didn't have his own gloves. But don't be fooled that this was a case of jack of all trades master of none – Newman brought quality to the back four and in midfield he showed he could play at a higher level but unfortunately for City it was not to be with them.

"I was born in Bradford-upon-Avon and was scouted by City's Jock Rae, a lovely man who is unfortunately no longer with us. I was playing at schoolboy level for City but it was touch and go whether I would be offered an apprenticeship. City were taking on 11 and they already had 10, then it got to me. Alan Dicks, Ken Wimshurst, Gerry Sharpe and Roger Quinton had to make the decision and apparently two liked me and two were not so keen. A tournament came up in France for us youngsters and I was invited to go. Unfortunately it clashed with one of my O levels but nothing was going to stop me in my dream of being a footballer. The tournament went well for me and on our return I was offered an apprenticeship. I never did find out who the two were who didn't fancy me."

The fall out from the Ashton eight debacle threw many of the City's youngsters into the Third Division relegation dog fight and Rob, along with many others, found himself in the first team at 18 but unfortunately it could not stop City's slide into Division Four.

"It was a really difficult time for the club and I think there was a real sense of relief that the club had survived. Obviously the eight had sacrificed their own careers so that we could have ours and I never forgot that.

"By the time I was 21 I had played over 150 games and us youngsters had got some great experience at a vital stage in our careers. We were in a win-win situation due to nobody expecting much from us. I remember going to Hereford and we were bottom of the Fourth Division. We had a squad of 14 but the team spirit installed by Terry Cooper was tremendous. We won 3-1 and it was a turning point for us. I think it was a night where we all became men.

"I have many derby memories and I loved playing in them, but the one I remember most was a league match in Division Three at Twerton Park. I had a great rapport with the City fans. They knew what I was about and how I loved the club and thank god they did because on that particular afternoon I missed a penalty and it has haunted me ever since."

A full house at Twerton saw City coming into the game three years since their last derby win and Rovers were definitely a side on the up. Supporters knew it was to be a battle when after 15 minutes City's Robbie Turner went up for a ball with Rovers' Geoff Twentyman resulting in the Rovers centre-half needing to go off for treatment to an eye wound that would need five stitches. City struck first in the 24th minute with a well worked move involving City's new £175,000 purchase from Leeds United, Bob Taylor, who had an impressive debut. Taylor passed to Chris Honor, who in turn fed the ball to Steve McClaren, whose shot struck a Rovers defender, only to arrive at the feet of Alan Walsh six yards out who put City one up.

But celebrations didn't last long: two minutes to be precise. Dennis Bailey chased a long ball which bounced off him and the City defenders straight into the path of Gary Penrice who drove the ball home.

City had numerous chances leading up to half-time with Taylor going close and Twentyman clearing an Alan Walsh shot off the line. Then with minutes of the first half remaining Yates was alleged to have pulled Taylor down in the box, so referee Phillip Wright pointed to the spot and awarded City a penalty.

"I was the penalty taker and although I had missed in the last game at Mansfield I stepped up to take it in front of the City fans. As I hit it Nigel Martyn went to his right and saved it. The City fans were silent but I could hear the roar behind me as the Twerton Park faithful went crazy. It was heartbreaking for me. I was a City fan and had the opportunity to put City in front and possibly win the game against the old enemy. We didn't say a lot at half-time in the dressing room and our manager Joe Jordan just told us to keep going as we were playing well. Nobody mentioned the penalty as they knew how I felt."

In the second half Newman had another effort superbly saved by Martyn. The game slowed down and chances for both clubs were few and far between, although Rovers nearly snatched it in the end when Waugh tipped a Penrice header over the bar and the game ended 1-1.

"I was gutted after the game. When I look back now I could've won it for City. The City fans were great to me. They knew what beating Rovers meant. I missed another penalty in the following game at home to Bury and I never took another for City but that one at Twerton hurt really bad."

Rob had 11 years at Ashton Gate captaining the club, won two promotions, played at Wembley twice in the freight Rover finals, made over 500 appearances and scored over 60 goals but he always had a desire to play at the very highest level and in 1991 the call from the Premiership came in the shape of Norwich City.

"I got a bit of stick for going to Norwich City. It was just after my testimonial and I had two years left on my contract but to be fair all City had to say was he's not for sale and they didn't, so I left for £600,000."

Rob spent eight years at Carrow Road which included playing in arguably Norwich's greatest game: a 2-1 away win against the mighty Bayern Munich in the UEFA Cup.

"It was a great night for the club and after the match I did think back to that game at Hereford and thought about how far I had come."

Rob finished up playing at Southend and later turned to coaching and management where he was boss at Southend, Cambridge and Bournemouth.

"Today I'm married and have a six year old daughter. I live on the south coast and still go to the City now and then and always get a good response from the staff and supporters. I'm looking to get back into management or coaching because I love it and want to test myself against the very best. I had a great career and have no regrets – well maybe one – a winning goal in a Bristol derby would've been nice."

When I interviewed Rob Newman for this book, it's testimony to him and his feelings for the fans at City in that he chose not a City win or a game in which he scored, but a game in which he felt he let the Ashton faithful down: a game that still hurts him today. The modern game needs young bright British coaches like Rob to come through and a chairman willing to believe in them so I'm sure whatever club is Rob Newman's employer in the future they will get the same man as the City fans got: Mr 100%.

Marcus Stewart

The best goal of my life

League Division One

13/12/1992

Bristol Rovers	**4-0**	**Bristol City**
Channing 22 mins		
Stewart 66 mins		
Saunders 67 mins		
Taylor 78 mins		

HT 1-0
Att 7,106

Bristol Rovers: Parkin, Alexander, Tilson, Yates, Hardyman, Browning, Channing, Stewart, Taylor, Saunders, Waddock, substitutes: Reece, Jones.

Bristol City: Welch, Harrison, Scott, Kristensen, Bryant, Osman, Shelton, Dziekanowski, Rosenior, Cole, Edwards, substitutes: Allison, Gavin.

On meeting Marcus Stewart you get a sense that there is no bigger critic of the highly acclaimed goalscorer than himself. Never one to offer excuses he shows an honesty and determination that is sadly lacking in some players of today.

Born in Hartcliffe, Bristol, Marcus' initial involvement with football was with Southampton football club.

"I was with the Saints at about 12 or 13 and they released me. At the time I was devastated but looking back it was the right thing for me. Within days of that disappointment I got a call from Roy Dolling at Rovers asking me to come to the club. I went, I loved it and signed as a schoolboy. Days later, Bristol City asked me to sign for them and although they were my team they were just too late."

Marcus went on to be one of Bristol Rovers' rising stars, scoring goals at youth team and reserve level, picking up 12 England youth caps along the way. On 17th August 1991, in Rovers' first game of the season at home to Ipswich Town he made his debut.

"It was a thrilling game. It ended 3-3 and I scored so my first team career hit the ground running.

"Obviously through youth team and reserves I had played City many times and I think my fourth senior game was against them away at Ashton Gate in the league where I think we lost 1-0. But the game I remember most is the 1992 game at Twerton, not only for the result, but because it was live on TV as well.

"We were managed at the time by Malcolm Allison and were on a bit of a roll so we felt really good. I remember he switched things round a bit and played with a new look diamond formation in midfield with me on the right side of it. When I look back he was really ahead of his time even then when he was in his 60s. We played fantastically and Justin Channing scored a cracking goal to put us one up at half-time. In the dressing room we knew we were playing well and couldn't wait to get the second half away."

Rovers continued the second half with their fluid football and City just couldn't get near them. In the 66th minute, a ball from the left was met on the volley by the young Stewart and it crashed into the top corner.

"I think my goal killed them off. It was the best goal of my life. As the ball came over I hit it and tried to put the ball into the opposite corner to the keeper and it flew in. I remember it hit a TV camera positioned just inside the net."

Minutes later, Rovers went three up through Carl Saunders and John Taylor made it four with 10 minutes left.

"At the final whistle the scenes were unbelievable. I remember being carried to the tunnel by fans. We knew how much this game meant to both sets of supporters so I remember thinking at the time, 'I won't score a more important goal than that'. It was strange being from the City side of town and at the time still living there and being a supporter as a young kid and here I was scoring against them. But I was a professional footballer and wanted to score against everybody no matter who they were."

The Malcolm Allison band wagon didn't roll on for very long and Big Mal found himself replaced by John Ward who became a mentor to the young Stewart and certainly brought out the best in the youngster.

"I liked John a lot. He was brilliant to me – a tremendous man and manager. I looked up to him and I still speak to him now for the odd bit of advice."

Marcus continued to score goals for Rovers and it wasn't long before a host of scouts were at Twerton to see him. Then in 1996 an offer from Huddersfield Town came along.

"I always wanted to test myself at a higher division. John had left and Ian Holloway was manager. He made it clear he wanted me to stay but I felt a move out of Bristol would do me good and would make me a better player. The easy option was to stay but I wanted to see if I could do it on a bigger stage which at the time Huddersfield were."

So Marcus left in 1996 for £1.2 million. He had scored 57 goals in 171 games for the "gas" and true to form hit the ground running in Yorkshire scoring a hat-trick in only his second game for the club, becoming a fans favourite. In 2000 after scoring 58 goals in 133 games he was controversially sold to rivals Ipswich Town on the final run in at the end of the season. Huddersfield fans were up in arms with new boss Steve Bruce but the deal went through.

"I had just come in from training and Steve said 'Ipswich Town want to sign you, do you want to go?'. To be honest if he wanted me he would've told Ipswich I wasn't for sale, so off I went and signed for George Burley."

At Ipswich, Marcus gained promotion to the Premier League via the play-offs and in the 2000/01 season he finished as the league's second highest scorer with 19 goals and secured the club a fifth place finish gaining a place in the UEFA Cup, and at the time there was a real push for him to be included in the England set up.

As now seems the norm with promoted clubs, Ipswich struggled in the second season and were relegated. Stewart moved to Premiership side Sunderland United.

"I think a lot of teams found us out in the second season at Ipswich and there were things happening behind the scenes after the relegation and I just found myself in and out of the team, so when I got the call out of the blue from Peter Reid I jumped at it. I spent three good seasons at the club and scored 31 goals in over 100 games. I was honest enough to realise that I could not play at Premiership standard anymore, so after a long chat with the then manager Mick McCarthy, who was great with me, I expressed a desire to move back to Bristol to fulfil an ambition to sign for City."

In 2005, under great expectations from the fans and local press Brian Tinnion brought Marcus to Ashton Gate.

"I was very excited to sign for the club. I was around 33 years old and felt I had a lot to give but I had to wait for my first goal and the club were low on confidence. I just didn't play well at City. People ask 'Was there a lot of pressure on you when you signed?' but I'm paid to handle pressure so that was no excuse. I just didn't do it for the club, the supporters and for myself and that's disappointing for me to say."

Brian Tinnion resigned and Gary Johnson took over and Marcus was not in his plans. So after a spell on loan at Preston United he signed for Yeovil and is now at Exeter City where he has just celebrated 250 career goals.

"I am enjoying my time at Exeter City and was 'Player of the Year' last year. I am also coaching the under 14's at Yeovil Town which was something I started to do while I was at the club and I love working with the kids.

"Of the future, who knows? I may stay in the game but you never can tell. I always thought throughout your career if you make more good decisions than bad then you will go on to have a good career and I think looking back that's what I did."

Andy Llewellyn

I *never had the best relationship with the gas*

League Division Two

05/03/1991

Bristol City	1-0	Bristol Rovers
Donowa 88 mins		

HT 0-0
Att 22,270

Bristol City: Leaning, Llewellyn, Bryant, Aizlewood, Scott, May, Shelton, Newman, Donowa, Taylor, Morgan, substitutes: Allison, Rennie.

Bristol Rovers: Parkin, Alexander, Twentyman, Clark, Jones, Mehew, Holloway, Reece, Pounder, Saunders, White, substitutes: Willmott, Sealy.

Andy Llewellyn was your typical no nonsense defender. He may not have had the skills and glamour of some of his team mates, but this hard-tackling passionate robin was Bristol City through and through and still is today.

As a youngster, Llewellyn was chased by a host of clubs which included Bristol Rovers, Manchester United, Aston Villa and of course his beloved Bristol City, so when it came to put pen to paper at schoolboy level there was only going to be one winner.

"I always wanted to play for City and it was a dream come true for me. The funny thing is when I signed as a schoolboy they were in Division One which then was the top flight but when I signed as an apprentice they were in Division Four after a succession of relegations sent the club into free-fall."

The turmoil at Ashton Gate at the time could not have been better for the young lad from Pucklechurch as he found himself playing first team football at the tender age of 16.

"I made my debut away at Rochdale in a 1-0 defeat in the 1982 season and it took off from there really for me. We had a host of youngsters and we were given our chance under Terry Cooper and it made men of us. I remember us being at rock bottom and we had to go to Hereford away. All the fans were in fancy dress it was a fantastic atmosphere. Terry Cooper had asked Chris Garland to help out and we picked him up on the way from Chepstow races. We won the match 3-1 and it was like turning a corner with the club. It was as if we could go no lower and from that match we went on a magical run and finished mid table. I will never forget Hereford away and people still ask me about it now."

Andy became a regular in the City side in the following years and that meant crossing paths with the rivals across the city on many occasions.

"I loved the derby games; they meant a lot to me and they meant a lot to the fans. They were always passionate affairs. I never had the best relationship with the gas supporters because they knew I was City through and through, but I never thought that relationship would end up with me in a police station."

The game was 1991. A packed Tuesday night at Ashton Gate. The atmosphere was electric. Both teams were mid table and only a point separated them. It was to be a game that tingled from start to finish and would end Rovers' five year dominance of the fixture.

"I remember before the match there was a minute's silence for former City chairman, Des Williams who had died a week earlier. To be honest the ground was silent and the majority of Rovers fans were respectful although you could still hear a few idiots shouting out but it just spurred us on and certainly added to the tension of the game."

City got at Rovers from the start and their build-up play was in a different class with Morgan going close twice and efforts from Donowa and Taylor almost finding the net. The game was played at extraordinary high tempo with City pressing and Rovers hoping for a chance on the break. With half-time looming Llewellyn was booked for a late challenge and Rovers' Alexander and City's May were forced off with injuries.

"We had battered them in the first half and our manager Jimmy Lumsden told us to keep going as we were on top but I had played in enough derbies where we had battered Rovers and they nicked it late on to be that confident."

In the second half, City continued to be on top with Shelton winning the midfield against a surprisingly quiet Holloway. Louie Donowa, a recent purchase from Ipswich for £45,000, was causing all sorts of problems for the Rovers back four with his runs, while City's Nicky Morgan hit the woodwork three times. Then on the 76 minutes mark, Aizlewood played a suicidal ball back to Andy Leaning in City's goal which Devon White pounced on. As White went round Leaning he caught the big striker and a penalty was awarded to Rovers.

"I couldn't believe it. We were so on top and I knew this would happen. I think I shouted a few choice words at Mark Aizlewood about the back pass."

With the City fans jeering, Ian Holloway stepped up to take the spot kick. He hit it strongly but Leaning guessed right and pushed it round the post. Ashton Gate went into raptures. I'm sure every City fan knew if Rovers had scored they would've taken all three points. It was to get better for the red half of the city 10 minutes later when after a mis-hit shot, Parkin in the Rovers goal failed to gather it and Louie Donowa stooped to head home his first goal of the season to secure a win for City.

"We went mental. It was right in front of the Rovers fans and we all jumped on Louie. We knew they wouldn't come back from it. The Rovers fans gave me stick all game so it was great to put one over them and I have to be honest I milked it for all it was worth.

"When the whistle blew it was like a promotion win. The Ashton Gate faithful were on their feet applauding

BARCLAYS LEAGUE DIV THREE
BRISTOL ROVERS
SATURDAY SEPTEMBER 12th. 1987 K.O. 3pm
OFFICIAL PROGRAMME 50p
TODAY'S MATCH SPONSOR: HIRE-RITE

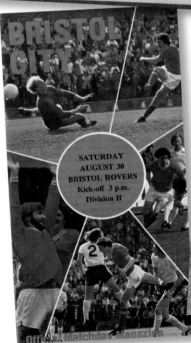

ABOVE: A selection of Bristol City programmes.

LEFT TOP: A formidable Bristol City line up from 1965 with Brian Clark 6th from right and John Atyeo 7th.

LEFT BOTTOM: An unusual shot of the 1965 Bristol City squad with the "old away end" in the background long before the Atyeo Stand.

ABOVE LEFT: Geoff Merrick.

ABOVE RIGHT: Martin Hirst.

RIGHT: The skilfull Keith Fear.

ABOVE: Bristol City's Alan Walsh celebrates another goal from a free kick.

LEFT: A youthful David Moyes.

ABOVE: Paul Cheesley.

LEFT TOP: Rob Newman of Bristol City.

LEFT BOTTOM: Donnie Gillies who played for both clubs.

RIGHT: Andy Llewellyn of Bristol City.

BELOW: Peter Beadle of Bristol City and one of the few to have played for both clubs.

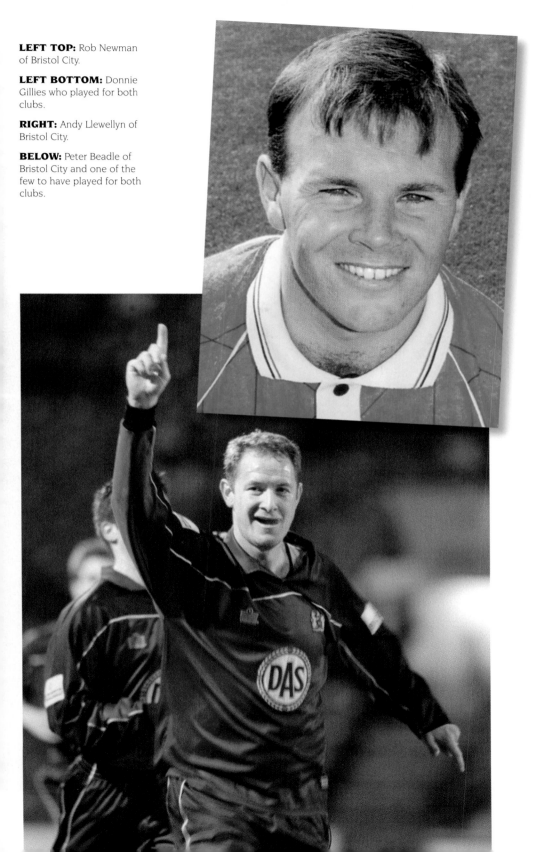

LEFT: An acrobatic Louis Carey clears the danger for City.

BELOW: Brian Tinnion with another killer pass.

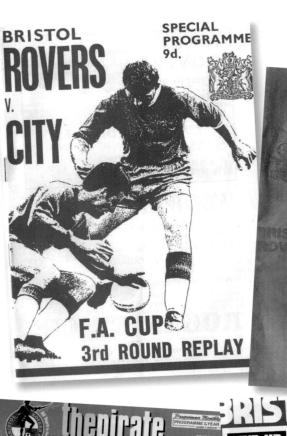

BRISTOL ROVERS v. CITY

SPECIAL PROGRAMME 9d.

F.A. CUP 3rd ROUND REPLAY

BRISTOL ROVERS

F.A. Cup – Round 2

GREAT MILLS
DIY SUPERSTORES & GARDEN CENTRES

Match Day Magazine – Price 50p

thepirate
The Official Match Programme of BRISTOL ROVERS FOOTBALL CLUB

SEASON 2006/2007
ISSUE NO 26
£2.50

PROGRAMME MONTHLY PROGRAMME & YEAR

bristol city
Johnstone's Paint Trophy
Area Final, 2nd Leg
Tuesday 27th February 2007
kick-off 7.45pm

BRISTOL ROVERS
SECOND DIVISION 1974-75

LINE UP

ROVERS –
Blue/White quarters

1 Jim EADIE
2 Phil BATER
3 Lindsay PARSONS
4 Peter AITKEN
5 Stuart TAYLOR
6 Jeff COOMBES
7 Martyn BRITTEN
8 Tom STANTON
9 Alan WARBOYS
10 Bruce BANNISTER
11 Gordon FEARNLEY
12

Referee:
G. W. HILL
(Leicester)

Linesmen:
W. H. SMALE (Barnstaple)
Red Flag

G. W. STOREY (Bridgwater)
Orange Flag

CITY –
Red/White

1 Ray CASHLEY
2 Gerry COLLIER
3 Brian DRYSDALE
4 Gerry SWEENEY
5 David RODGERS
6 Geoff MERRICK
7 Trevor TAINTON
8 Tom RITCHIE
9 Paul CHEESLEY
10 Kevin GRIFFIN
11 Jimmy MANN
12

MATCH NO. 15
DIVISION II
Saturday, December 28th
Kick-off 3 p.m.

PRICE 10p

OFFICIAL MATCH-DAY MAGAZINE

ABOVE: A selection of Bristol Rovers programmes.

LEFT: Peter Hooper with that trusted left foot.

BELOW: Peter Hooper.

BOTTOM: Paul Randall scores one of his two goals in the 1984 FA Cup derby win.

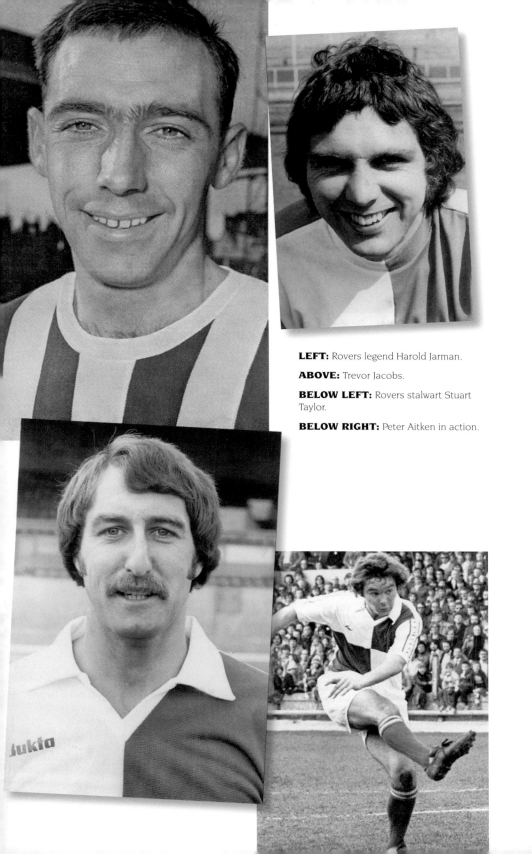

LEFT: Rovers legend Harold Jarman.

ABOVE: Trevor Jacobs.

BELOW LEFT: Rovers stalwart Stuart Taylor.

BELOW RIGHT: Peter Aitken in action.

RIGHT: Tony Pulis.

BELOW: Carl Saunders of
Bristol Rovers in action.

ABOVE: David Mehew 'Boris' of Rovers.

ABOVE: Marcus Stewart during his time at Rovers.

ABOVE: Geoff Twentyman in a typical Rovers move!

and to give Rovers their due, the supporters stood and clapped their team off the pitch as well.

"The next day I was woken by a phone call from boss Jimmy Lumsden at 8.30am in the morning. He told me to get myself to the ground quick as the Avon and Somerset police wanted to interview me. I thought it was a wind up, but I went to the club and myself and Rob Newman had to go to Broadbury Road police station to be formally interviewed. They asked me where I was last night at 9.40pm. I said I was playing at Ashton Gate and asked what is this about? The police officer told me I had been reported for obscene gestures to the Rovers fans after the goal. He apologised and said it had to be investigated and it could go to court. So myself and Rob were hauled before a disciplinary hearing at the FA, but there was no evidence for the FA and the police so it was all dropped. My recollection of the incident is that if I did make any gestures to the Rovers fans, it was because I was on such a high, although that is no excuse. To be honest, I really can't remember."

Andy went on to play for City for 12 years but then after falling out with new manager Russell Osman he was let go by the club.

"I was heartbroken. I never wanted to leave the club. I went on loan to Exeter and Hereford then eventually joined Yeovil but if I'm honest I just missed City so much I didn't want to be anywhere else. I had played over 400 games for the club and retired aged 29 which was no age when I look back."

Today Andy plays for Keynsham Town in the western league and works in Weston-Super-Mare as a postman which he's done for 10 years. He still goes to Ashton Gate and gets a great response from fans. I met him for this interview at Bristol City's academy, where one of his sons has just started playing for the club. So who knows, maybe City fans have not seen the last of a Llewellyn in a red shirt.

Carl Saunders

Just like the old days

League Division One

13/12/1992

Bristol Rovers	4-0	Bristol City
Channing 22 mins		
Stewart 66 mins		
Saunders 67 mins		
Taylor 78 mins		

HT 1-0
Att 7,106

Bristol Rovers: Parkin, Alexander, Tilson, Yates, Hardyman, Browning, Channing, Stewart, Taylor, Saunders, Waddock, substitutes: Reece, Jones.

Bristol City: Welch, Harrison, Scott, Kristensen, Bryant, Osman, Shelton, Dziekanowski, Rosenior, Cole, Edwards, substitutes: Allison, Gavin.

I interviewed Carl Saunders for this book at Bristol Rovers' Memorial Ground. We met outside the club shop on a wintery Friday afternoon and proceeded to the warmth of a back office to start the interview. A couple of minutes into it, there was a knock on the door and a very apologetic lady from the Rovers asked if Carl could sign a couple of things after he finished for some supporters who had seen him arrive. "No problem" Carl said "I will do them now". On further inspection we were greeted by a group of men around early thirties whose eyes lit up like they were 14 again. "Thanks Carl you're a top bloke, always smiling just like the old days at Twerton", they shouted. It was wonderful to see at first hand the affection still felt for this likeable former Rovers star who was part of a golden time for the club.

Born in the Midlands, Carl signed as a YTS trainee with Stoke City and made his debut in the top flight against Everton aged 17.

"Apparently I was the first YTS trainee in the country to play top flight football and I did really well at Stoke. I had a great rapport with the fans and I had eight great years there but Alan Ball took over from Mick Mills in 1990 and after scoring 24 goals in 164 games I was no longer in his plans.

"Numerous clubs came in for me including Bristol City and Bristol Rovers. I didn't know too much about Bristol but both clubs had managers with a good footballing pedigree in Gerry Francis and Joe Jordan. I knew whoever I signed for I would learn a lot from and would hopefully become a better player. I talked it over with Alan Ball and he sold me Bristol Rovers as a club and Gerry Francis as a coach as he had been at the club as a player and knew Gerry very well. When I first met Gerry I couldn't believe what a genuine down to earth guy he was; he was like your friend and he instilled such great belief in your own ability. But when I went to the ground I thought, 'Oh my god'. No disrespect to Bath City but I couldn't believe Twerton when I saw it. I thought 'We are never going to play there are we?', and as for the training ground: a chocolate factory? I was dumbstruck. The whole set up on the outside looked so amateurish but on the inside the club was so professionally run it was untrue."

Carl made his debut for Rovers in a 1-0 victory away at Preston North End and a week later scored two goals on his home debut in a 2-0 victory against Walsall and as if things couldn't get any better, he scored the first hat-trick at Twerton in Rovers' 6-1 demolition of Wigan a week later.

"I was on fire! So were the team. We had such a great spirit at the club from tea lady to manager and we all worked for each other. I think the fact that people thought we were 'rag bag Rovers' made us stronger. That season culminated in us achieving the Third Division title beating Bristol City along the way. I know people will expect me to pick the famous 2nd May match: the night we secured promotion by beating City 3-0, and obviously it's a game I will never forget, but the game I remember with even fonder memories was in 1992 at Twerton when we beat City 4-0. I had played City many times and had played in derbies for Stoke City against Port Vale and they are always passionate affairs and this was no different. Gerry had left the club to go to QPR and we had had Martin Dobson in charge. It was a disaster that only lasted 12 games. We then had Dennis Rofe who was with us a year but was sacked in the November. It was a difficult time for us and we didn't know what to expect and when our new manager walked in and it was Malcolm Allison we couldn't believe it. I was looking forward to working with him as he was a legend in the game and I remember the derby he was in charge mainly for the fact that every goal was a cracker."

Rovers went into the game with the Malcolm Allison revival rolling on from the previous four game. They had taken seven points from a possible 12 and with Allison installing a new diamond formation to midfield Rovers were in confident mood to face their neighbours. An 11th minute challenge from City's Gerry Harrison on Marcus Browning sparked a 20-man brawl in the centre circle and Harrison was lucky to escape with a yellow card. The game settled down and both sides caused each other problems with City going close with Andy Cole and Rovers' Justin Channing just firing over. Rovers broke the deadlock on 22 minutes when Channing picked the ball up 30 yards from goal and let fly with a shot that beat City keeper Welch and went straight into the top corner. They went into the interval one up and deserved their lead in the second half. Rovers turned on the pressure and a 15 minute spell meant the end for City. On the 66th minute, a cross from the left by Rovers' Hardyman was met by Marcus Stewart on the volley and he cracked it home. City were shell shocked and it got worse a minute later when Saunders picked the ball up 25 yards out and hit a rocket that Welch in the City goal got nowhere near.

"I remember in training Malcolm saying to us that when you strike a ball strike it with the laces and boy did I strike that one. We had City penned in their own half and everything we did came off. I didn't want the game to end."

Rovers wrapped it up on the 78th minute when Waddock dispossessed Dziekanowski in midfield and pushed the ball to John Taylor whose low shot beat Welch at the far post to end City's nightmare.

"The final whistle was fantastic. I remember myself and Marcus Stewart being carried aloft by the fans to *the tunnel. I will never forget the joy on the fans' faces."*

The Allison revival didn't last and Big Mal left in the February of 1993. Steve Cross took over for a couple of games before John Ward was installed as manager in the March.

"My contract was up for renewal and I didn't really figure in John's plans and Rovers decided to let me go. It wasn't the way I wanted to leave the club. I had scored 42 goals in 142 games. To be honest when I look back at my time there I do get very frustrated particularly when I think of the Championship side. I feel when Gerry left we should've appointed someone who knew the club inside and out, maybe someone like Geoff Twentyman who could've pushed us on and knew the fans, after all they were our 12th man. They will never know how important they were to us that season but having said that I am so proud to be part of their history."

Carl had spells with Oxford United, Walsall and also played in Malta. After retiring from football he joined Avon and Somerset constabulary as a community affairs co-ordinator and also works for Bristol Rovers as their community liaison officer.

"I now work in the community and often get recognised which is great. I even get City fans say they hated me when I played for Rovers which just shows I did my job. I always get a good response from the people at Rovers and yes, I'm still smiling, just like the old days."

Louis Carey

It was a defining moment in my career

League Division Two

16/01/1996

Bristol City	**0-2**	**Bristol Rovers**
		Beadle 73, 75 mins

HT 0-0
Att 20,007

Bristol City: Welch, Carey, Mcleary, Paterson, Edwards, Hewlett, Owers, Kuhl, Tinnion, Maskell, Nugent, substitutes: Barnard, Bent, Agostino.

Bristol Rovers: Parkin, Channing, Clark, Tilson, Armstrong, Gurney, Browning, Matthew, Miller, Stewart, Beadle, substitutes: Sterling, Higgs, Wright.

In this modern era of football where from Premiership to Blue Square league fans feel they have no affinity with the players of their club, Bristol City's Louis Carey is a rare commodity: a local boy captaining his local club.

As we sit overlooking the car park at Bristol City, it's hard not to see the rewards of the modern footballer: Bentley's, Merc's and BMW's are neatly parked around the players entrance and it would be easy to think that players of today don't really care about the game that brings them such riches.

But on spending time with City's skipper you get a real sense of a lad who cares deeply for his club and the responsibility which lies with being captain of a team he followed as a young boy.

Signed as a schoolboy, Carey secured a YTS contract after an away game for the youth team at Gillingham.

"After returning to Bristol, Dave Bell, the youth team boss told me in the car park at Ashton Gate that I was to get a YTS contract. Joe Jordan was in charge and I was so happy. It was all I ever wanted to do. After that Joe Jordan offered me a one year pro deal in 1995 and gave me my debut away at York City and I never really looked back in terms of playing in the first team. My memories of playing Rovers was that they were always big games. Even when I was in the youth team we had some right old battles with them but I remember we always beat them.

"The game I really remember though was probably my first derby game at a senior level. It was at Ashton Gate, January 1996, a fantastic evening game. Matches at Ashton Gate under floodlights were really *special and a game against Rovers just added to the atmosphere. Joe Jordan was in charge and he really fired us up as he knew what it meant to the supporters but to be honest winning meant everything to me too."*

Bristol City started well and looked the more enterprising early on. Matt Hewlett had a shot finely saved by Parkin and on the 13th minute, Beadle turned on a throw-in from Armstrong and steered the ball across the goal for the oncoming Gurney to just miss contact. Hewlett again caused Rovers problems when he met a Kuhl free kick but had his header well saved. City then had their best chance of the half when Brian Tinnion played the ball to Craig Maskell. Hitting a cracking shot, Parkin could only push it to the oncoming Nugent and as the whole of Ashton Gate held its breath, Rovers' Miller came from nowhere to dispossess him on the line and stop City from going 1-0 up as the 45 minutes came to an end.

Either team could've gone off at half-time in front but it remained 0-0.

After the interval, City forced five corners in 13 minutes and began to take control. A killer ball from Tinnion sent Hewlett free but his shot just went wide. On the 73rd minute, Rovers' Andy Gurney robbed Edwards in the City midfield before surging into the box. His shot came off Welch's chest but Gurney passed the rebound across the goal to Beadle to put the ball in an empty net which put the gas 1-0 up. Two minutes later Paul Miller played the ball on the edge of the box and Beadle crashed a spectacular strike into the goal and won it for Rovers.

"I couldn't believe it. We were so on top and in the space of a couple of minutes we were 2-0 down and chasing the game. I remember going to take a throw-in just in front of the Dolman Stand and the City fans were going ballistic. I could see on their faces how they were feeling. They weren't angry with us as players just with the way it was going. It's a memory I will always have: you really did see what a defeat would mean to them. With us chasing the game I remember they broke away on us and I think it was a three against two situation. I made a tackle on the edge of the box and even though we were getting beat, our fans applauded it. It was a defining moment in my career, a game against our rivals and I knew I could do it on the big stage. The game ended 2-0 and I was gutted to have lost but I had a good game. The next evening I had to go to an Evening Post awards function at a hotel in Bristol. Ian Holloway and Peter Beadle were there and were brilliant to me, telling me that I had a bright future in the game and that meant a lot to me."

Louis went on to play over 300 games for Bristol City and after missing out on the play-offs in 2004 he was out of contract and had the chance to join Coventry City.

"I would've signed for City but the opportunity to play at a higher level was too much to resist. Coventry had just come down from the Premiership and they had a new stadium. Peter Reid was in charge in 2004 so I signed."

Carey was in and out of the side at Coventry playing only 27 games. He received a call from his old team mate Brian Tinnion who wanted him back now that he was manager.

"I signed for City in the January and it was the best birthday present I ever had. Putting that shirt on again was an amazing feeling. I feel very lucky to have had the chance again but to be captain is the ultimate honour for me. I'm not one of those captains who shout and scream; that's never been my style.

I would rather lead by example and the lads know I'm always there for them if they want a chat."

Louis has gone on to be part of a very successful Bristol City side with promotion and just missing out on the Premiership under the guidance of Gary Johnson.

"The gaffer has been fantastic to me and we knew when he came he would do well for us. He has the respect of the players and there will be some good times at the club with him here. As for me, I want to stay fit and lead this club to success. The supporters are everything to me at this club; they have always given me a great reception and I am aware of my responsibility to them.

"On a personal note I'm getting married in 2009 and with a future father-in-law who is a big Rovers fan, the Bristol derby will always be special to me."

Peter Beadle

I'm glad I took the challenge

League Division Two

22/12/2000

Bristol City	**3-2**	**Bristol Rovers**
Millen 49 mins		*Bignot 1 min*
Beadle 55 mins		*Cameron 78 mins*
Thorpe 74 mins		

HT 0-1
Att 16,696

Bristol City: Phillips, Carey, Millen, Hill, Murray, Clist, Tinnion, Brown, Bell, Peacock, Thorpe, substitutes: Beadle, Amankwaah.

Bristol Rovers: Culkin, Bignot, Jones, Foster, Thomson, Hogg, Pethick, Cameron, Ellington, Evans, Bryant, substitutes: Meaker, Astafjevs.

Peter Beadle is a very rare breed when it comes to Bristol football: he's a player who played for both clubs at the height of his career and still, to this day, continues to be thought of with affection by both the red and blue half of the city.

Born in Lambeth, London in 1972 the young striker was picked up by Gillingham and made his debut, aged 17, after showing much promise with the Kent club. He earned a dream move to Premiership side, Tottenham Hotspurs, in 1992 but never made a first team appearance and left to join Watford in 1994.

"The move to Spurs was fantastic for me. I supported them as a boy and learned so much while I was there. The facilities and the coaching of Terry Venables was top class and I was surrounded by players such as Sol Campbell, Terry Sheringham and Darren Anderton but unfortunately I wanted to play regularly and that would mean a move away so Watford seemed ideal. But again I found myself in and out of the side and it became very frustrating for me until I played a reserve game against Bristol Rovers on a Tuesday night at Vicarage Road.

"We won 5-1. I scored and within the week John Ward at Rovers made an offer for me. I agreed to speak to John and to be honest when I walked into the club it was the first real club that just felt right to me. There was something about the place. I knew I would do well and the whole move was a big thing for me. I was married with two kids and it was a real test to move away from Kent where I was living but as I said, it just felt right."

So in 1995 Beadle moved to Twerton Park and his career at the "gas" took off like he thought it would.

"I made my debut against Wycombe Wanderers away in a 1-1 draw and played really well. I got a good response from the gas heads as well."

In fact Peter got 12 goals in 27 appearances that first season including two in the 2-0 win at Ashton Gate against Bristol City.

"I can honestly say I loved the derby matches and always seemed to do well in every one I played in. I remember the first derby I played in when I scored twice, it was a dream night. The match on Sky TV at Ashton Gate the following year was also a game to remember. I got Rovers' equaliser and there was a pitch invasion; we had to run off the pitch. When the ref stopped it I couldn't believe what was going on. I remember it wasn't a great advert for the Bristol derby and it made all the papers but for the wrong reasons.

"I loved my time at Rovers and scored 43 goals in the two and a half years I was with them and I think looking back doing well in the derby matches really built up the relationship I had with the fans. I left to go to Port Vale who were in the Championship at the time and I remember talking to the Rovers manager, Ian Hollowa,y who told me: 'It's a challenge and unless you try you will never know how good you can be', so off I went. The move didn't go well; there was a change of manager and I found myself in and out of the side. Then out of the blue the new manager, Brian Horton, told me he had got an offer from Notts County and I ended up at Meadow Lane with Sam Allardyce in charge and did really well. We were struggling when I joined them but things got turned round. Then Sam left to go to Bolton and there was massive upheaval at the club and I was on the bench and was told I was to be put on the transfer list. To be honest it was just one of those things. I enjoyed my time at County and met some lovely people at the club and was sad to leave. Out of the blue an offer came in from a couple of clubs and the biggest shock was that one of them was Bristol City.

"I thought long and hard about it. I had a choice of three clubs: City, Rovers and my first club Gillingham so to be honest the easy move would've been Gillingham or Rovers but I wanted to challenge myself and I could only do that at City. You have to remember I was an ex-Rovers player signed by a manager the fans didn't like, Tony Pulis, because of his Rovers links so it really should've been the last club I'd join but I always believe you have to challenge yourself to find out about yourself."

So in 1999, Peter Beadle, the thorn in the side of Bristol City on numerous derby matches, signed for the reds.

"I made my debut at Ashton Gate in a 1-1 draw against Colchester and it went well. I never really got slaughtered by the City fans but obviously had my critics and although the team at the time were struggling in Division Two they were really good to me; I appreciated that and I think they knew it took balls to sign for them. It's because of the City fans that the derby match I remember most was a game where I think they finally accepted me as a player and a game where I finally earned their respect. It was 22/12/2000 at Ashton Gate. That season had been frustrating as I hadn't played many games. Tony Pulis had left and Danny Wilson was in charge and at the time Tony Thorpe and Lee Peacock were occupying the front two spots and doing well so my chances were limited to the subs bench but I never doubted my ability and knew I would get a chance at some point."

And that night in front of the live Sky TV cameras Beadle got his chance. A packed Ashton

Gate, along with thousands of armchair football fans watching TV at home, saw a great footballing advert for Bristol football.

The match sprung to life in the first minute when a ball from Simon Bryant was flicked on by Nathan Ellington and Marcus Bignot charged behind a sleeping City defence and lofted the ball over Steve Phillips in the City goal to put Rovers 1-0 up. The gate was silenced except for the thousands or so gas heads jumping for delight in the old East End. City were stunned into action and minutes later a header from City captain Millen went inches over from a Tinnion free kick. Both teams were clearly fired up for the game with tackles thundering in from both sides and it wasn't long before Rovers' Evans found himself in referee Clive Wilkes' notebook for a rash challenge on City's Louis Carey which left the City youngster laid out for a few minutes. On the 16th minute, City almost equalised when Mickey Bell went on a run but his cross just missed the oncoming Thorpe. Both teams created chances and the 1-0 score at half-time didn't do both teams justice.

The second half had barely started when Beadle came on for the injured Peacock. Lee took a knock in the first half and at half-time he said he would see how it was second half but the moment he got out there he signalled to the bench and on Beadle went. The switch couldn't have been better as within minutes Beadle linked with Scott Murray and his cross was headed in by City captain Millen to make it 1-1. Six minutes later, Mickey Bell found Beadle unmarked in the box and with a perfect cross the ex-pirate smashed a header into the Rovers net to make it 2-1 to the City.

"It was a wonderful moment. The whole of the Atyeo Stand were singing my name and I think they thought 'Well he's been here two years and worked his socks off and hasn't complained about not being in the side so fair play to him'. I will always remember that moment."

After the goal Rovers boss Ian Holloway made some changes bringing on Meaker and Astafjevs for Evans and Ellington but Beadle was having a stormer and nearly scored again when his goal-bound shot was superbly saved by Culkin in the Rovers goal. There was no let up for the visitors and it got worse. In the 74th minute, Thomson needlessly gave the ball away and it was picked up by Aaron Brown who was having the game of his life in midfield and his cross was met by Tony Thorpe to put City 3-1 up. Rovers replied minutes later when after a mistake by Louis Carey, Hogg fed Martin Cameron and his shot beat Phillips to make it 3-2. City quickly awoke from the setback and Beadle almost made it four with his shot just grazing the post in the dying minutes. The match finished 3-2 and Ashton Gate had seen one of the great local derbies and the neutrals at home had seen a fantastic advert for football in the South West.

That season City finished ninth in the league whilst Rovers were relegated. As for Peter, he went on to score five goals from only 20 games and the following season after injury he was released by the club.

"I loved my time at City; they were a great club for me and I'm glad I took the challenge. I am so proud of what I achieved at both Bristol clubs and the response I get nowadays if I go back to either is really good. The fans always ask who I preferred and I always say Spurs!"

After leaving City in 2003 Beadle had brief spells with Brentford and Barnet before joining non-league side Team Bath in June 2004. He became player-commercial manager at Clevedon Town and in 2005 was appointed manager of Conference South club Newport County where he had a successful spell until he was dismissed in April 2008.

Today Pete is living in Gloucester and is hoping to get back into football in either management or coaching. One thing is for sure, if there's any chairmen out there who want someone not frightened of a challenge, then Peter Beadle is your man.

Steve Phillips

Balls of steel

Johnstone's Paint Trophy Southern Final First Leg

21/02/2007

Bristol City	0-0	Bristol Rovers

HT 0-0
Att 18,370

Bristol City: Basso, Carey, Fontaine, Keogh, Orr, Johnson, Noble, Woodman, Murray, Andrews, Brooker, substitutes: Jevons, Skuse, Myre-Williams, Artus, Thomas.

Bristol Rovers: Phillips, Lescott, Hinton, Elliott, Carruthers, Igoe, Campbell, Disley, Haldine, Lambert, Walker, substitutes: Nicholson, Sandell, Ogi, Lines, Green.

People say footballers and particularly goalkeepers need tremendous self belief and balls of steel, well in Steve Phillips' case his career has, to date, shown he has both in abundance.

Steve Phillips was born in Midsomer-Norton in 1978 and as a schoolboy he found himself in goal due to his older brothers and the well laid out family garden.

"When I used to play football out in our back garden we had two trees which made a perfect goal and my brothers would bully me into going between the sticks whenever we played and that's how it all started. I got into Poulton Rovers' first team at about 17 years old and was playing in the Screwfix league and it was a tough old league especially for a young raw keeper, which I was.

"I went to Plymouth Argyle for two weeks on trial but it didn't really work out and then Poulton got a call from Bristol City to say they were interested in having a look at me. I went to City for the week and played for the reserves against Swansea and we won 8-0 and I never touched the ball. The week was a real eye opener for me. I worked with Stuart Naylor, Keith Welch and Mike Gibson and they taught me so much and showed me what was needed to make the grade. After the week, City invited me to play another reserve game, this time against Swindon Town at Clevedon, which we won 3-2 and City offered me a year and a half deal. I was so pleased I resigned from my job as a printer in Poulton and they too were so happy for me as they knew it was what I really wanted, but I knew I would have to really work hard to make the grade as it was a massive step up in class. I did work really hard and finally made my debut in a 2-0 home victory against Sheffield United.

"I will always remember it. The fans were brilliant and we were struggling at the time in the Championship with Benny Lennartsson in charge. I had a good game and at the end City's Terry Connor ran over to me and gave me a big bear hug and said 'That's how you make your debut my son'. I was 20 and made the keeper's shirt my own and went on to make over 300 appearances for the club through good times and bad, in fact I played for five managers in that time."

But then in 2005 Bristol City manager Brian Tinnon resigned and Gary Johnson took the hot seat at Ashton Gate and after 10 years with the club Steve didn't figure in the new manager's plans.

"It was made pretty obvious to myself and a few other players that we had no future at the club. Football is all about opinions and I accept that but things were said about me in the press that just weren't true and it hurt me that the supporters who I had given everything to for the best part of 10 years believed that rubbish about me throwing my dolly out of the pram. It was a difficult 14 months for me; I was in the reserves and I was even substituted from some reserve games and all I wanted to do was play. There were offers from Huddersfield and Danny Wilson at Milton Keynes Dons but City wanted money for me and clubs were looking for a free transfer.

"It was difficult and without the support of my friends and, most importantly my family, I don't know how I would've got through it. Then after being 14 months without a first team game, Rovers came in with an offer and I found myself crossing the City to play for the 'gas'. No disrespect to the Rovers but I would've gone anywhere and I think that's what hurt about the City fans thinking I had done it deliberately. Rovers were the only ones to offer a fee and I just wanted to play first team football. My career had gone backwards at City but even so I didn't feel it was a good way to leave a club I had had 10 great years with and had a lot of affection for, but as a player, you just want to play.

"I was really excited to join them and the thought of first team football again renewed my enthusiasm for the game. Paul Trollope and Lennie Lawrence were a different class to me and I was a bit apprehensive regarding how the fans would take to me. I remember saving a penalty against them in the 2000/01 season deep into injury time and as a result of that game they were relegated. So City fans always sang 'Phillips sent the gas down' and obviously these things went through my mind before I signed but they welcomed me with open arms."

Steve continued to play well for Rovers and put the problems he had at City behind him until fate played a cruel twist.

"We had beaten Shrewsbury in the Johnstone's Paint Trophy; the final whistle blew and we were through to the area final and our opponents were going to be Bristol City. I stood in the goal mouth and thought 'Oh my god'. I didn't really want to play Bristol City for the next three years let alone three months after leaving them. The build-up to the game was all about me which may have helped other players but it just added to the pressure on me and again, things were said about me in the press, obviously with a view to unsettling me but I knew it would happen and I just focused on the game. Going back was hideous. We were on the bus with a police escort. As we got off at the players entrance there were about 200 people shouting 'Judas!, Judas!' and all sorts of other things. That's when I knew I was in for a rough ride.

"The atmosphere was unbelievable. I have played in lots of big games with both clubs: play-off finals etc, but the pressure on me that night was like nothing I had ever experienced. I knew I had to be at my best and that we needed balls of steel, and by god we had them. That night at Ashton Gate was unbelievable and I will remember it for as long as I live.

"The City fans sung songs about me all night and although the game was certainly no classic, I played text book goalkeeping: my catches from crosses, my kicking and decision making were top draw and for us to come away from Ashton Gate with a 0-0 draw I knew the team could go all the way and finish the job at the Memorial Ground."

Six days later Rovers did finish the job in front of a capacity 11,550 crowd with a Rickie Lambert strike sending Rovers to a final at the Millennium Stadium against Doncaster which they unfortunately lost.

"Again, the night at the Memorial Ground was fantastic although I do regret dropping my shorts in the dressing room for the cameras as we were celebrating. I think some City fans thought it was aimed at them but that couldn't be further from the truth. It was aimed at someone but I won't say who. Although I was ecstatic to get to a final, I can honestly say I did feel strange knocking out a team I had great affection for; a team that helped turn a raw, local lad into a player; a team I had spent 10 years at and had highs and lows with. I still had some great mates at the club."

Steve continues to be the number one keeper at Bristol Rovers and has won many awards at the club including Player of the Year and the football league's Golden Gloves award for most clean sheets for the 2006/07 season.

And of the future?

"I would like to play on for as long as I can and maybe one day go into coaching. On a personal note, I am married and have a young son and I hope to be a support to him as my dad has been to me throughout my life. Who knows, I might even plant two trees out in the back garden."

Brian Tinnion

I *danced around the corner flag*

League Division One

06/04/1993

Bristol City	2-1	Bristol Rovers
Morgan 35 mins		Taylor 81 mins
Tinnion 79 mins pen		

HT 1-0
Att 21,854

Bristol City: Welch, Munro, Osman, Aizlewood, Bryant, Tinnion, Allison, Shelton, Pennyfather, Rosenior, Morgan, substitutes: Harrison, Thompson.

Bristol Rovers: Kelly, Alexander, Yates, Tillson, Clark, Mehew, Reece, Waddock, Pounder, Stewart, Taylor, substitutes: Channing, Evans.

People say that modern footballers don't care, but you only have to spend time with Brian Tinnion to realise how much this likeable Geordie loved and cared about Bristol City, and how one night in a Bristol derby, the "Tinman" would become a fans' favourite forever.

Born in Stanley, County Durham in 1968, Brian was brought up watching Newcastle United with his dad and like all those other thousands watching he dreamed of one day putting on those famous black and white stripes. An outstanding youngster with a tremendous left foot, Brian's dream came true and he was signed as an apprentice with the north east giants. He became a member of the Newcastle United FA Youth Cup winning team of 1985, a team that included a certain Paul Gascoigne, and a bright future beckoned under the guidance of Newcastle manager Jack Charlton.

"*I signed my first professional contract a few days before my 18th birthday on the pitch at St. James' Park before a home game. It was an incredible feeling.*"

Brian went on to play 32 games for the magpies and scored two goals in his left-back position, but unfortunately for him after Jack Charlton left and former keeper Ian Mcfaul was sacked as manager, Jim Smith arrived at the club and made it plain he wanted experience in all positions and Brian found himself looking for a new club.

"*I was disappointed but Jim was a good bloke and I didn't want to sit in the reserves, especially as I had tasted first team football. I had two offers: one from Middlesbrough and one from Bradford City. I liked Terry Yorath, the manager at Bradford and he sold me the club; they were in a higher division so I joined them.*"

Brian went to Bradford City for £150,000 in 1989. It was at Bradford that Brian was pushed up to play in midfield and became the creative player we all remember. He was an instant hit with the fans particularly when in 1990 he scored a last minute penalty against rivals Leeds United to earn Bradford a point in a heated local derby.

"I enjoyed my time at Bradford City and I had four good years there. I was coming to the end of my contract and we couldn't agree on a new one. Unbeknown to me Bristol City's chief scout Tony Fawthrop's son was a regular at Bradford City and he told his dad all about me and how my contract was up and next thing City made an offer and it went to a tribunal."

In March 1993 Brian moved to Bristol City for the controversially low tribunal fee of £180,000. He had played 145 games for Bradford City and scored 22 goals.

So, a love affair with Bristol City started...

"I didn't know a lot about Bristol. I had come down before I signed and watched a game with Tony Fawthrop. I liked the way they played; the crowd was great and I had a really good feeling about the place. I couldn't wait to sign and I made my debut away in a West Country derby against Swindon Town. The atmosphere was great although we lost 2-1. I loved the passion of the fans but I have to say it was nothing compared to my fourth game for the club."

And it is that fourth game that Brian will always remember: a home game against bitter rivals, Bristol Rovers.

"I had been used to derby matches at Newcastle and Bradford but I couldn't believe this night. In my view it was bigger than anything I had been involved in before. The build-up of the media and expectations of the fans was immense. Both clubs were struggling at the bottom half of Division One and nobody could afford to loose. It was a packed evening game and I think 5,000 were locked out of the ground. They delayed the kick-off by 15 minutes; it was crazy. I remember saying to the lads 'Is it always like this?', and they said 'Welcome to Bristol Brian'."

Both teams started well and it was obvious this was to be no dull 0-0 result. Rovers' John Taylor went close when his shot just went wide after a mistake by Matt Bryant. City switched from their original sweeper system to a traditional flat back four which seemed to suit them more and on 34 minutes the breakthrough happened. Player-manager Russell Osman pumped a long free kick forward but Rovers' defenders went to sleep and allowed Wayne Allison to get behind them with a diagonal run. His cross was collected by City's Nicky Morgan in acres of space; he controlled it and blasted the ball into the Rovers net to put City 1-0 up and send the "gate" into raptures. City continued to run the game and could've gone 2-0 up minutes later when Allison had a volley superbly saved from Kelly in the Rovers goal. The noise of "drink up ye cider!" was almost halted just before half-time when Keith Welch in the City goal saved a shot from Rovers' Andy Reece.

"We went in at half-time 1-0 up and were quite confident but knew they would come at us second half. I was pleased with my performance and as a team we had all had a good first half but knew it would count for nothing if we let them back in it second half."

With Rovers desperately needing something out of the game everybody expected them to throw everything at City in the second half but their lack of firepower saw Marcus Stewart substituted for Evans and there only seemed to be one team who would get the next goal and that was City.

On 79 minutes the inevitable happened: Tinnion's pass saw Allison racing forward on the right. His early cross saw Leroy Rosenior's close range effort saved by Kelly in the Rovers goal only for the rebound to fall to Tinnion whose shot was handled on the line by Rovers' full-back Ian Alexander. Referee Mike Reed had no choice but to send Alexander off and award City a penalty.

"Martin Scott, our penalty taker, was suspended and everybody just looked around. I had taken penalties for Bradford and just thought 'Sod it, I'll take it'. I picked up the ball and I knew where I was going to put it and I crashed it into the top corner. The noise as it hit the net was incredible. I ran from my team mates and I danced around the corner flag to celebrate before I became engulfed in red shirts."

To Rovers' credit they didn't give up and on 81 minutes striker John Taylor hit a shot that beat Welch in the City goal after some good work from substitute Evans. But it was too late for Rovers and on the final whistle the City supporters went crazy.

"I will never forget that night. We had champagne in the dressing room and it was bedlam. I really knew what a Bristol derby was after that."

City finished that season mid table but Rovers were relegated after finishing bottom. It was an incredible derby match and must rank up there with the best.

After securing himself in the hearts of City fans Brian went on to gain cult-like status with the City faithful with his performances and his obvious love of the club. Brian became one of City's dominant players of the 1990s. He switched from wide on the left to centre of a three-man midfield under manager Danny Wilson in 2000 and his form led to him being voted best player in his division by the PFA. This also culminated in him becoming player-coach in 2000.

"I loved the coaching. I had worked with the youth team in the 90s and had become a bit of a father figure to some of the young lads at the club. I was a great buffer for Danny as lads would speak to me before him. I would also do various functions in the community if Danny couldn't make it and I loved meeting the fans. Danny was very good to me. He trusted me a lot and he would ask me when I wanted to train. We got on very well."

City made good progress under Wilson, culminating in a play-off final against Brighton in 2004. Unfortunately for all the thousands of City fans who made the trip to the Millennium Stadium in Cardiff that May afternoon, City were awful and lost 1-0 which led to Wilson being sacked.

"I can't explain why we didn't perform and I was really sorry to see Danny go and next thing I knew chairman Stephen Lansdown asked me to be the manager. I thought long and hard about it and I knew it was early but the only thing that scared me was that I was worried I would never get the chance again to manage the team I loved. I agreed and got a call from Danny to wish me well and to tell me how hard it would be and my god was he right. All my mates were in that dressing room and now I was the boss.

I know most of them deleted me from their phones as they realised we had a different relationship now."

So Brian's managerial career with City started at Torquay United with a 1-1 draw and in his first season Brian guided City to seventh: just outside the play-offs.

"To be honest the job was damn near impossible for me. It was so difficult going from mates with the lads to boss and although we had a good first season I felt I needed an older head to help me. I had tried to get Joe Jordan back at the club to help me and Terry Connor who was a great number two but we couldn't get anyone in."

Brian's problems at City came to the boil seven games into the 2005/06 season with an away game at Swansea City.

"We had terrible injuries and I had to play half the youth team. Chairman Stephen Lansdown had a chat with me on the morning before we left and said 'Look I know we have terrible injuries and everything is stacked against us today but just try and go out and do your best. Get what you can'.

"With five minutes before half-time we were at 0-0, then we let one in and in the second half we just fell apart and lost 7-1. I remember looking at them. We had no leaders on the field and we had nothing on the bench to change it. If I had been able to play that would not have happened as I wouldn't have let it. The defeat hurt me so much and still does to this day and it upset me more that I could see it hurt me more than some of the players. So at the end I just sat in the dug-out and rang my wife and told her that it was all over. I even asked her to come and get me as I didn't even want to go on the bus home with them. Unfortunately she couldn't and it was a very long journey home, but my mind was made up. I met Stephen Lansdown on the Sunday morning and he was great. He said 'Tell me what you want, I will get anything you need, I will back you 100%', but I had had enough and I left."

Brian had played 458 games for City and scored 36 goals. As a manager he won 11, drew 9 and lost 14.

"When I look back I should never have taken the job. I should've gone away and got some experience and then maybe come to the club. It hurts when I think about how I left. Maybe with hindsight I could've weathered the storm and come through it. Stephen Lansdown certainly thought I could but that's football. I just wanted to do well for those fans."

After leaving City Brian kept fit by training with his old boss John Ward at Cheltenham Town. He also played a few games for another old team mate Martin Kuhl who was at Aldershot. Then he got a call from Charlton Athletic to run some soccer schools for them in Spain.

"I still had the disappointment of City and I thought, 'Why not?'. So we all moved to Malaga in Spain and it went really well, then Charlton had financial problems so I set up my own soccer schools and they're going really well. I have even been offered a job with CD Alhaurino who are in the Spanish Third Division as a coach and that's ongoing at the moment, so I'm sure it won't be long before I step back into management again. I'm older and wiser now and when I look back at my time at City I always think of that night when I won the fans over with that derby penalty. It really was the start of a wonderful relationship."

Trevor Jacobs

I'm proud to have played for both clubs

Gloucester Cup Final

29/04/1974

Bristol City	**0-2**	**Bristol Rovers**
		Staniforth 12 *mins*
		Rudge 23 *mins*

HT 0-2
Att 15,986

Bristol City: Cashley, Sweeney, Drysdale, Gow, Collier, Merrick, Tainton, Mann, Cheesley, Fear, Gillies, substitute: Ritchie.

Bristol Rovers: Eadie, Jacobs, Parsons, Aitken, Taylor, Prince, Fearnley, Stanton, Warboys, Rudge, Staniforth, substitute: Dobson.

Look at any successful football team and it will have its fair share of unsung heroes. The Bristol Rovers promotion side of the 1973/74 season had one such man and that was Trevor Jacobs. While everyone remembers Warboys and Bannister's "smash and grab" exploits of that season, the input of the tough tackling ex-Bristol City full-back should always be remembered.

Born in Bedminster, Bristol, the young Trevor was a prolific goalscorer for Bristol Boys and was soon signed by Fred Ford's Bristol City, beating off stiff competition for the youngster from Everton, Manchester City and of course, Bristol Rovers.

"I was a local lad and City were my club so I was always going to sign for them, but to be honest at that early age my ambition was just to play for the first team: it didn't matter if it was only one game, the ambition was to put on that red shirt."

Trevor progressed through the ranks at City and was switched to full-back early on. It was a position he revelled in.

"I enjoyed playing full-back. I could tackle and I was quick which meant I could get up and down the wings and cross a ball. The coaches worked on my defensive awareness and it worked; they obviously saw something in me at that time."

Trevor made his debut for City in a thrilling 3-3 draw against Rotherham United where City came back from 3-0 down but Trevor was credited with an own goal. Not the best of starts for a youngster on his debut.

"To be fair the ball struck me on the way to the net and there was nothing I could do, but I really enjoyed the game and did very well. I learned an awful lot playing at that level and the lads were great to me."

Jacobs went on to secure his position in the City side becoming a regular under Fred Ford.

"I enjoyed my time at City particularly the games against Rovers. I had done battle with them over many years from schoolboy to first team and I loved playing in those games; they were games you just didn't want to loose. I remember the late chairman of City, Harry Dolman, saying to the squad once 'I don't care what you do all season, just beat Rovers in the Gloucester Cup'. I never lost a game for City against Rovers and as I said, they were really special games for me and the supporters and being from Bristol only added to the match."

With the departure of Fred Ford and the arrival of Alan Dicks as manager of City, Trevor found himself in and out of the side and in 1972 he was loaned out to Plymouth Argyle.

"I think as a player when you're put out on loan the writing really is on the wall for you. It's obvious you don't figure in the manager's plans, after all I was no youngster trying to get experience I was one of the seasoned pros at the club then so I wasn't happy towards the end. The situation was resolved by City giving me a free transfer and I was due to sign for Hereford but when I got a call from Rovers manager Don Megson he really sold the club to me. He told me they had just sold Phil Roberts to Portsmouth so there was a vacancy at right-back; he told me they were on the up. It was a dream for me. I didn't have to move my family and I was at a club that wanted me. I wasn't quite certain what the reaction of the fans would be towards me crossing to the old enemy but I just thought, 'Whatever happens I'm going to have to start well for the 'gas' to get the supporters on my side'."

So in the season of 1973/74 Trevor joined the Rovers. He had played 131 games for City and scored three goals. He made his Rovers debut away at Bournemouth in a 3-0 win.

"After the sad way it ended at City I couldn't believe how things went for me at Rovers. The supporters were great. I never missed a game, and we won promotion. It was the happiest season I had ever had in my career. As the season was drawing to a close I couldn't help thinking of the Gloucester Cup on the horizon. We were due to meet City at Ashton Gate and to be honest if we beat them it would be the icing on the cake for me."

Rovers travelled to Ashton Gate on 29/04/1974 full of confidence as they had just won promotion to the Second Division and during the season they had gone on a 32 match unbeaten run. City on the other hand had finished 16th in Division Two and had enjoyed a Cup run that had seen them beat the mighty Leeds United at Elland Road. The atmosphere at the game was like any other Bristol derby. You couldn't pick between both sides and the noise from both sets of supporters was incredible.

"It was great to go back as part of a winning side. I really felt I had a point to prove and was desperate for us to do well. I remember getting stick when I came out to warm up and got quite used to the calls of 'City reject, City reject', but I expected it and just got on with my game."

Rovers started well and showed the confidence that had won them promotion with John Rudge going close early on. Then on the 12th minute, a slack back pass by Gerry Sweeney to Gerry Gow was intercepted by Rovers' Frankie Prince which sent Gordon Fearnley off down the right. His cross bounced off City keeper Ray Cashley's chest, only for Rovers' Staniforth to blast the ball home. It was no more than Rovers deserved. City were playing 4-4-2 and Rovers had three in midfield with John Rudge spare, relishing his freedom. City did go close when debutante Jimmy Mann sent a shot just wide of Eadie's post on the 20th minute but Rovers continued to boss the game and on 23 minutes, Warboys put a short pass to Rudge and let fly from 20 yards out and left Cashley stranded to make it 2-0.

"We went in at half-time and we knew we had won it. City hardly had a shot and to be honest I was surprised by City as they just hadn't turned up in the first half. We expected more from them in the second half."

In the second half, both teams cancelled each other out. There were few chances but Rovers had shut the game up and on the final whistle the blue and white fans were ecstatic whilst the red half of the city poured out of the ground. Rovers captain Stuart Taylor picked up the Gloucester Cup and topped off a perfect season for the "gas", and of course for Trevor Jacobs.

"The win meant so much to me. From a professional point of view it gave me an opportunity to show a few people at City that they were wrong to let me go and that was a very satisfying feeling. On a personal note I was a Bedminster boy and always had a soft spot for City. They were my club and I know the supporters gave me stick but they don't always get the full facts of why a player leaves, they just think it's a slight against their club and to me it was only ever about playing first team football and feeling wanted by a club."

Trevor continued to be a popular player at the Rovers and in 1976 he made a decision to retire.

"I was 30 years old and physically in really good nick. I always wanted to go into business and I just thought I would get out while I was at the top. I went in to see Don Megson and told him. He wished me well and the club paid up my contract and that was it."

Jacobs had played 82 games for the Rovers and had scored three goals. He then went into the pub trade taking a pub in Shepton Mallett and later one in Whitchurch.

"Things went well for me. I moved into the management side of things and did a bit of coaching at the Rovers with the young kids as well which I loved. I did get very disillusioned with the game when I went to take my coaching badge with Phil Bater of Rovers. The chap taking us was an obvious school teacher who had never kicked a ball in anger and I remember one of the sessions we were doing was full-backs defending. When he told Phil and myself we were doing it wrong we both told him in no uncertain terms that our way was the right way, but he told us if we wanted our badges then we did things his way. Looking back I think that says it all: how the FA were in turmoil regarding coaching at that time. Things went down hill with the pub trade and I ended up looking for a job. I bumped into former City keeper Mike Gibson who was working for the post office and he got me an application. I joined about 20 years ago and have loved it ever since. When I look back over my career, I only have one regret and that was that I retired too early. I could've gone on for at least another five years but other than that I'm proud to have played for both clubs and the reaction I get from City and Rovers fans now makes me even prouder."

David Moyes

I have had some good times in my life and Bristol City is one of them

Freight Rover Trophy

16/12/1986

Bristol City	**3-0**	**Bristol Rovers**
Newman 25 mins		
Walsh 54 mins		
Moyes 56 mins		

HT 1-0
Att 6,903

Bristol City: Waugh, Newman, Moyes, McPhail, Williams, Marshall, Fitzpatrick, Hutchinson, Walsh, Neville, Riley, substitutes: Moore, Llewellyn.

Bristol Rovers: Carter, Hibbitt, Jones, Carr, Tanner, Penrice, Alexander, Smart, Noble, Morgan, Purnell, substitutes: Scales, Mehew.

There is a familiar saying in life that "It's not how you start it's how you finish", and that couldn't be more apt when applied to the career of former Bristol City centre-half David Moyes, a man who cut his managerial teeth coaching Brunel Glazing in the Bristol Sunday league.

As I sit in his office at Everton's new £15 million state of the art training facility on the outskirts of Liverpool, surrounded by Manager of the Month awards and messages on his pad to "phone Sir Alex back" and "Rafa called", I can't help feeling rather proud that this tough Scot, Bristol City fans will remember with affection, has made it to the very top in today's ruthless world of football. I feel even more proud when he talks about his affection for the city of Bristol.

Born in Glasgow in 1963 the young Moyes was always going to be a footballer.

"I was spotted as a youngster and signed by Celtic. It was a dream come true for me. I went through the ranks and Billy McNeill gave me my debut. I spent three years in the first team and won a Championship medal in the 1981/82 season. Then out of the blue I got an offer to join Cambridge United down in England. I thought long and hard about it and decided to test myself south of the border."

So in 1983 Moyes joined Cambridge United on a free transfer but after only two seasons he again found himself up for sale.

"*Things were OK at Cambridge but I was in and out of the side and when Terry Cooper and Clive Middlemass came in for me I jumped at the chance. I have to say I didn't know too much about Bristol but I did know it had two clubs.*"

Moyes joined Bristol City in 1985 for £10,000 and made his debut in an away game defeat at Meadow Lane against Notts County but as with Cambridge, he found himself in and out of the team at first.

"*I struggled at first but we had some great lads at the club. People like Alan Walsh, Rob Newman, Keith Curle and fellow scot Bobby Hutchinson all helped me a great deal and after a while it just clicked for me and I never looked back. When I think about it now I could tell you the whole team off the top of my head, we had a real special bond amongst us and were on the up as a club and Terry Cooper was a great influence on me at that time.*"

David was part of a team on the up. In his first season at the club they got to Wembley for the first time in their history playing Bolton Wanderers in the final of the Freight Rover Trophy, beating them 3-0. It was the following year in that competition that David remembers his favourite game against Bristol Rovers.

"*I always enjoyed the games against Rovers and I got a few goals in them too. They were always intense affairs with both clubs giving 100%. I remember the match in the Freight Rover Trophy, mainly because I was under pressure for my place at the time as Terry Cooper had brought John McPhail in from York City earlier in the season and all the speculation was that he was going to replace me. A crowd of only 6,903 turned out at Ashton Gate for a tournament that only captured the public's imagination in the later rounds but non the less it was a Bristol derby. Even though Ashton Gate was not at capacity we knew what it meant to the 6,000 or so in the ground and they made a noise worthy of 20,000. City fielded a very experienced side and that couldn't have been further from Bobby Gould's Rovers team that was full of youngsters.*"

Rovers survived an early onslaught with City's Bobby Hutchinson going close and to their credit Rovers themselves could've taken the lead after 15 minutes when Garry Smart, a player who six months earlier was playing park football, missed a sitter at the far post. The let off seemed to give City the kick up the backside they needed and on 25 minutes a header from City's Bobby Hutchinson fell to Rob Newman where he smashed the ball into the Rovers net to put City 1-0 up. More goals seemed inevitable from City but Rovers survived, particularly due to Rovers' player-coach Kenny Hibbitt who cleared a shot from Neville off the line. As the teams went off at half-time, although Rovers were only 1-0 down, the gulf in class was evident for all to see.

After the break City continued to bombard the Rovers goal but young Tim Carter, the Rovers keeper, held out but only until the 54th minute. A right-wing cross from Marshall was helped on by City's Glyn Riley. As it came to Alan Walsh he spun round and hit a cracking strike to the top corner to put City 2-0 up. Two minutes later, David Moyes took advantage of a poor clearance by the Rovers defence. He looked up and crashed City's third into the back of the Rovers net.

"*I must admit it was great to score against Rovers. It was my fifth of the season and I think a goal against the local rivals always brings you a bit closer to the fans.*"

City sat back for the last 20 minutes and almost let Smart in to snatch one back for the "gas" but Keith Waugh in the City goal saved well. As the whistle blew it was plain to see that City had a nucleus of a good team and Rovers had some rebuilding to do under Bobby Gould's management.

City went on to get to Wembley in the final of the Freight Rover Trophy against Mansfield but unfortunately drew 1-1 after extra time, and lost on penalties with Gordon Owen and David Moyes missing their crucial shots.

"I remember practising non-stop on the training ground so when I came to take mine I was very confident. I remember hitting it straight down the middle but the keeper, Kevin Hitchcock, saved it with his legs. I never took a penalty ever again after that. As for the derby game, I have been involved in many through my career with Celtic and Everton, even Preston. I don't think anyone can say one is bigger than the other as they all mean so much to the supporters and are tremendous to be involved in, especially when you win."

As David's career progressed at Bristol City he always had an eye on coaching and to his credit he was willing to start with a Sunday football team.

"I got asked by somebody at the club who was a friend of a friend if I would help out Brunel Glazing as a coach so I said 'Yes'. I really loved it and the lads were great and we had some good laughs. It's funny now when I think it was literally my first coaching job but I can't remember if it's on my CV. I always wanted to do coaching and I used to help out with the Bristol City schoolboys at the time and really enjoyed it. Most of the lads at that time would tell you I was a born organiser in and around them so it's probably no surprise I got into management.

"Things were going well for me at City when suddenly they brought in John Pender at centre-half and Terry Cooper told me I just wasn't in his plans anymore. I was bitterly disappointed. I had just bought a flat in the Clifton area of Bristol and I loved it at the club. I didn't want to leave. I have great respect for Terry Cooper and Clive Middlemass, even though when I see them today I tell them they were wrong to have let me go."

Moyes moved to Shrewsbury for £30,000 in 1987. He had played 83 games for the "robins" and scored six goals. He was at Shrewsbury for three seasons and played over 96 games for them before a free transfer back to Scotland came knocking with Dunfermline and then Hamilton. Then in 1993 he was signed by Preston North End again on a free transfer where he went on to play over 150 games before being asked to become manager after the departure of Gary Peters. A successful time at Preston, where the club enjoyed promotion and various play-off finals, led him to being noticed for his talents by the big clubs and in 2001 after the departure of Walter Smith, David left Preston to take charge of Everton football club, where he has been for the last eight years, making them one of the top six sides in the Premiership and making him one of the best managers in the game.

"I have had some good times in my life and Bristol City is one of them. It was without a doubt the best time of my playing career. I really loved the club and when I have been back I have been touched by the good reception I get from the crowd. I always wanted to manage the club and I can't go into details but one time I was very close to being the manager at City but it was not to be."

It's safe to say that David Moyes would not feature in a list of Bristol City greats. It's true he was a first class centre-half and in his defence he was only at the club for two years. But the people of Bristol City football club, the supporters and in general the people of Bristol, have never been forgotten by Moyes. As he plies his trade at the very top of football's elite and every season he builds on his own reputation, he is a lesson in hard work and dedication and an example to any aspiring coach. He certainly has come a long way.

David Mehew

We were all in it together

League Division Three

02/05/1990

Bristol Rovers	3-0	Bristol City

White 25, 55 mins
Holloway 62 mins pen

HT 1-0
Att 9,813

Bristol Rovers: Parkin, Alexander, Twentyman, Yates, Jones, Mehew, Holloway, Reece, Purnell, White, Saunders, substitutes: Nixon, McClean.

Bristol City: Sinclair, Llewellyn, Newman, Humphries, Bailey, Gavin, Rennie, Shelton, Smith, Morgan, Turner, substitutes: Honor, Ferguson.

People may be surprised at my choice of David Mehew for this book. Yes I could've gone for Holloway, Penrice or White when thinking about that great Championship winning team but I wanted to speak to a player I regarded as an unsung hero of that side. A player I don't believe had a better season than the one where Rovers became the top team in the city.

David Mehew was born in Camberley, Surrey 29/10/1967. As a talented youngster he was with Queens Park Rangers.

"I was at Rangers but I never signed anything and was just enjoying my football. I remember playing in a county match at Molineux and I was spotted by a Leeds United scout. It was fantastic really as I was a mad Leeds United fan and I couldn't believe it when they signed me. Within weeks I was training with all those great players that I used to idolise. Eddie Gray was manager and Peter Lorimer was his assistant, I really had to pinch myself sometimes."

Although David worked hard with the club he didn't get offered a contract and was released. But as luck would have it, Leeds United chief scout Tony Fawthrop was travelling over to Holland to see some matches and he was feeling rather sick on the ferry when he got talking to Bristol Rovers' manager at the time Bobby Gould, who himself was suffering at the hands of the rough seas. Tony told Bobby that two lads were very unlucky not to get contracts at Leeds which were defender John Scales and midfielder David Mehew and typical Bobby when he got home signed them both.

"I didn't know much about Bristol to be honest but I just wanted to play football so the move was

great for me. I was 18 and couldn't wait to get started. My first game was as a sub in a 6-1 defeat at Bournemouth. It was quite funny really as Bobby sent me on and said 'Go on son, make something happen'. I must admit I didn't make a lot happen. That season I made four sub appearances and went on loan to Bath City which was great for my confidence. I scored regularly for them.

"In the meantime Bobby Gould had left and was replaced by Gerry Francis. Things were going well for me and players like Geoff Twentyman, Ian Holloway and skipper Vaughan Jones were pestering Gerry to bring me back from loan to get me in the team. I will always be grateful to them for that."

So at the start of the 1986/87 season David made his debut in a 3-0 win at Walsall.

"I was glad to get my start and I did well. It was also about that time I got the nickname 'Boris', after Boris Becker who had just won Wimbledon due to my blonde hair; a nickname that has stuck ever since, and I really felt part of a team.

"The rivalry with City was always there. They were games you didn't want to loose. I played in loads of derby matches and have some great memories. I even played in goal in one at Ashton Gate when our keeper Tim Carter was injured. I made a few saves and kept a clean sheet although the boys in the back four really did protect me until Tim came back on. We didn't really go out socially with any of the City boys but I did know City's Mark Gavin from my days at Leeds and always got on well with him, but he did have a way of rubbing people up the wrong way. I will never forget being out in Bristol and Mark was throwing his money about winding myself and a few other Rovers players up by saying 'Look how much our win bonus is'. We never forgot it. Those comments found their way back to the dressing room particularly in the build-up to the biggest derby Bristol had witnessed in recent times."

Rovers and City were at the top of the Third Division and not only battling it out for promotion but the Championship too. Going into the game, if Rovers won and kept their unbeaten home record they would be promoted but if they lost they would hand the Championship to rivals City. Twerton Park that night would be no place for a neutral.

"I remember the day of the match Gerry didn't have us in to train or anything he just left us to our own devices and I was just walking round the house like a caged animal. In the end, I went and played on the pitch and putt at Warmley with a mate to kill the time. Anyway I bumped into the Bristol referee Roger Milford whose house backed onto the course. He was with a friend of his. I said 'Hello' and they wished me all the best for the game and said they would both be there.

"The atmosphere on that hot May night was unbelievable. I don't think I had ever seen Twerton so full. When we walked out I couldn't believe the noise. It was then I noticed the referee, Roger Dilkes, and it was the guy I had seen earlier in the day. No wonder he said he would be there. I must admit it did make us laugh."

Both teams started cautiously but it wasn't long before Rovers got into their stride and really took the game to City. On the 15th minute a ball was played for Mehew to chase with City's Andy Llewellyn and on winning it, Mehew pushed the ball back for Phil Purnell to strike it just over the City bar. Then to every "gas" head's delight Rovers got the break they needed: Holloway hit a ball into the box and it came out to Mehew on the right wing. He crossed but the ball hit a City defender and it came back to him. He then crossed again and the ball found Devon White in the box and the big centre-forward crashed it home in front of the travelling City fans behind Sinclair's goal. The Rovers faithful went crazy and their chorus of "Goodnight Irene" was only interrupted by the sound of Mr Dilkes' whistle for half-time.

"We knew we had them beat. They never had a kick first half and we were playing the best football we had played all season. Nobody in that division could've lived with us the way we were playing. Gerry just told us to keep it going and carry on where we had left off first half."

Rovers did exactly that. A ball crossed into the box from Ian Alexander was met by Carl Saunders and his header just glanced wide. City replied minutes later with an attack of their own when a cross from Gavin was met by Dave Rennie but his header was saved by Parkin in the Rovers goal. Rovers piled on the agony for the red half of the City on 55 minutes when Carl Saunders turned Rob Newman and as the City defender lost his footing, Saunders passed the ball back to White who cracked home his and Rovers' second to leave City dead and buried.

City had hardly got out of their own half and the whole Rovers team seemed to have the bit between their teeth. Maybe it was a culmination of always being the so-called "rag bag Rovers" or maybe being in City's shadow but this was a game they were never going to loose. On 62 minutes the "gas" put the game beyond doubt. A ball hit into the City box for Devon White to jump for with Sinclair the keeper and City full-back John Bailey fell to Purnell who shot towards goal. It was hit off the line with his arm by Andy Llewellyn. The rebound fell to David Mehew who headed the ball home but the referee gave a penalty to Rovers for the hand ball and the game was stopped for around 10 minutes while Bailey received treatment from the medical staff as it seemed in the collision he had swallowed his tongue and he was substituted for Chris Honor.

Meanwhile at the other end, the City fans were not too pleased with the impending defeat and some of them pulled off hoarding signs and proceeded to throw them at the row of police that had now lined the touchline behind the City goal. To his credit City manager Joe Jordan went to try and calm some of the supporters down. After the ensuing melee there was still a penalty to take and up stepped Ian Holloway to drive the ball home to send Rovers into the Second Division.

"I will never forget the final whistle. It was mayhem and it will live with me forever. We had to fight our way off the pitch and we all went into the stand to receive the adulation of the fans who were now on the pitch. We all sang 'Goodnight Irene'. Those fans were a real part of us. We were a family club and we were all in it together. Later that night all the players went to Chasers night club in Kingswood except me. I think it was the first time I hadn't been to Chasers on a Wednesday night for weeks. I went home to my family and prepared for the last game of the season a few days later away in Blackpool, but I have to say I missed a great night. I'm only sorry the lads didn't bump into Mark Gavin."

The following Saturday 5,000 "gas" heads descended on Blackpool and had the time of their lives as Rovers won 3-0 with Mehew getting one of the goals to clinch the title. City also gained promotion after winning 4-0 at home to Walsall but Rovers had become top dogs.

It was a remarkable achievement for the Rovers. Gerry Francis had taken a bunch of players who were probably not the most gifted. They were players who had been released by certain clubs, but he turned them into a team with a never-say-die attitude and a side with an incredible team spirit. A team that will always be remembered by the Rovers faithful as one of the club's great sides.

As for "Boris", he continued to be a regular for the "gas", even after the departure of Gerry Francis and the breaking up of that great side. Managers came and went and in 1993 John Ward joined the club.

"I worked really hard in pre-season and was looking forward to playing with some of the youngsters the club had brought through like Marcus Stewart and Marcus Browning. I don't think I had been fitter, however I then got an injury in pre-season and that was it. I went out on loan with Exeter City only because John wanted to see me play but the injury was too bad. My knee just ballooned and that was the end for me. It was really frustrating as I didn't get the opportunity to show John Ward what I could do, so I left. I had been at the club for nine years but didn't get a testimonial which was disappointing."

David Mehew had played 222 games for Rovers and scored 63 goals. He won a Championship with the club and also played at Wembley in the Leyland Daf Cup for them. He is also the last Rovers player ever to score at Eastville, all be it a reserve game against Watford, but these are things he is intensely proud of.

After leaving Rovers, "Boris" went to Walsall for a year where he won promotion for them. He also had a spell with Northampton Town and soon moved into non-league football plying his trade at various clubs including a return to Wembley with Forest Green Rovers in the FA Trophy final.

Today Dave is a rep for a stationary company and is also the manager at Gloucester City where he is starting to carve out a successful career in management. He still has links with Rovers as his two sons Olly and Tom are with the Centre of Excellence.

"I am very proud of my Rovers career and my time in the Bristol derby games. They were really special to me and the fans were incredible. They really did make every game a great atmosphere to play in, particularly that famous night in May."

Final Thought

So what of the Bristol derby today?

There are those who question the Bristol footballing public's appetite for the fixture especially with the demise of the Gloucester Cup final, a game that always commanded full houses for the end of season showcase and towards the end of its run had gates of fewer than 4,000 spectators at either ground.

You can say there are many factors that have changed the look of the Bristol derby, for instance the demise of local lads in either teams, although to be fair to both clubs this is a problem throughout British football. You also have to look at the violence the fixture has produced on the terraces over the years; how sad that many supporters will go to every game except the one against their fiercest rivals for fear of trouble.

Obviously when we look back on the Bristol derbies of old, particularly when we were young, we can't help but look with rose coloured spectacles. I do feel sorry for the young fans of today; they will never have the Peter Hooper of their generation going to the match with them on the local bus or a modern day Donnie Gillies chatting with them on a Saturday night in their local about the day's match. Today's supporters feel alienated by the modern player. Some live in gated communities and drive past fans in their blacked out Bentleys refusing to sign autographs for fear of it ending up on an internet auction site. I don't want to hang the modern footballer out to dry, it's just the way the game has gone and I wonder what happened to it, particularly when a team like Gretna FC in the Scottish League can go bust for £40,000 and a modern player can spend that amount on a watch.

Maybe we get the players we deserve and by that I mean who can blame them not being out and about with the supporters? Years ago players from Rovers or City could go to either ground on their night off and watch their rivals play and have a bit of banter with the supporters or go for a drink, and chat to the bar man about football. Now some players have to be careful where they go socially with their families and their only crime is that they play for City or Rovers. Who wants to run the gauntlet of some idiot trying to impress his equally drunken mates by screaming abuse at a player when he's out with his family just because he earns X amount of pounds or missed a sitter on Saturday? It's a sad reflection on our own society.

So is there any hope?

Football is growing at an incredible rate with wages out of control which doesn't appear to be about to change, unless a big club goes to the wall. The game is as popular as ever and the media cannot get enough of it. How ironic it is that if you were a supporter before Italia 90 you were regarded as some kind of hooligan yet now everybody has to have a favourite "footy" team to support and in the middle of all this lies our own Bristol derby. Both clubs work very hard in the community and the players play their part by being involved. The relationship between the two is very healthy; I can vouch for that with their cooperation with this book.

I long for them to be in the same division so supporters can support the fixture as they showed in both JPS semi-finals that had Ashton Gate and the Memorial sold out for both ties. Both teams also have excellent youth policies and can't fail to produce local lads that will no doubt be the stars of future derbies, but what will keep this fixture alive and special will be the fans, they should never forget that.

Throughout the pages of this book players of every era have spoken about the atmosphere and the passion of the fixture all provided by the fans on the terraces. The Bristol derby belongs to us, the people of Bristol. Let us celebrate it and place it up there with the best in the world. That's the least it deserves.

Neil Palmer

Bristol Derbies

League Matches

1898
Western League
Bristol Rovers 2-3 Bristol City (16/03/1898)

1899
Southern League Division 1
Bristol City 1-0 Bristol Rovers (26/12/1899)

1900
Southern League Division 1
Bristol Rovers 1-0 Bristol City (13/04/1900)
Bristol City 1-0 Bristol Rovers (20/10/1900)

1901
Southern League Division 1
Bristol Rovers 1-1 Bristol City (08/04/1901)

1922/1923
Division Three (South)
Bristol City 0-1 Bristol Rovers (23/09/1922)
Bristol Rovers 1-2 Bristol City (30/09/1922)

1924/1925
Division Three (South)
Bristol Rovers 0-0 Bristol City (25/10/1924)
Bristol City 2-0 Bristol Rovers (28/02/1925)

1925/1926
Division Three (South)
Bristol City 0-0 Bristol Rovers (07/11/1925)
Bristol Rovers 0-1 Bristol City (20/03/1926)

1926/1927
Division Three (South)
Bristol Rovers 0-5 Bristol City (09/10/1926)
Bristol City 3-1 Bristol Rovers (26/02/1927)

1932/1933
Division Three (South)
Bristol City 3-1 Bristol City (15/10/1932)
Bristol Rovers 1-1 Bristol City
(29/03/1933)

1933/1934
Division Three (South)
Bristol City 0-3 Bristol Rovers (26/08/1933)
Bristol Rovers 5-1 Bristol City (30/12/1933)

1934/1935
Division Three (South)
Bristol Rovers 2-2 Bristol City (05/09/1934)
Bristol City 1-1 Bristol Rovers (06/02/1935)

1935/1936
Division Three (South)
Bristol City 0-2 Bristol Rovers (07/09/1935)
Bristol Rovers 1-1 Bristol City (04/01/1936)

1936/1937
Division Three (South)
Bristol Rovers 3-1 Bristol City (05/09/1936)
Bristol City 4-1 Bristol Rovers (02/01/1937)

1937/1938
Division Three (South)
Bristol Rovers 1-0 Bristol City (28/12/1937)
Bristol City 0-0 Bristol Rovers (30/04/1938)

1938/1939
Division Three (South)
Bristol City 2-1 Bristol Rovers (22/10/1938)
Bristol Rovers 1-1 Bristol City (25/02/1939)

1946/1947
Division Three (South)
Bristol Rovers 0-3 Bristol City (28/09/1946)
Bristol City 4-0 Bristol Rovers (01/02/1947)

1947/1948
Division Three (South)
Bristol Rovers 0-2 Bristol City (27/09/1947)
Bristol City 5-2 Bristol Rovers
(14/02/1948)

1948/1949
Division Three (South)
Bristol Rovers 3-1 Bristol City (18/09/1948)
Bristol City 1-1 Bristol Rovers (05/02/1949)

1949/1950
Division Three (South)
Bristol Rovers 2-3 Bristol City (10/09/1949)
Bristol City 1-2 Bristol Rovers (14/01/1950)

1950/1951
Division Three (South)
Bristol City 1-0 Bristol Rovers (02/09/1950)
Bristol Rovers 2-1 Bristol City (30/12/1950)

1951/1952
Division Three (South)
Bristol City 1-1 Bristol Rovers (15/09/1951)
Bristol Rovers 2-0 Bristol City
(19/01/1952)

1952/1953
Division Three (South)
Bristol Rovers 0-0 Bristol City (20/09/1952)
Bristol City 0-0 Bristol Rovers (07/02/1953)

1955/1956
Division Two
Bristol City 1-1 Bristol Rovers (22/10/1955)
Bristol Rovers 0-3 Bristol City
(03/03/1956)

1956/1957
Division Two
Bristol City 5-3 Bristol Rovers (22/09/1956)
Bristol Rovers 0-0 Bristol City (02/02/1957)

1957/1958
Division Two
Bristol City 3-2 Bristol Rovers (12/10/1957)
Bristol Rovers 3-3 Bristol City
(05/04/1958)

1958/1959
Division Two
Bristol Rovers 1-2 Bristol City (01/11/1958)
Bristol City 1-1 Bristol Rovers
(21/03/1959)

1959/1960
Division Two
Bristol City 2-1 Bristol Rovers (10/10/1959)
Bristol Rovers 2-1 Bristol City (27/02/1960)

1962/1963
Division Three
Bristol Rovers 1-2 Bristol City (15/09/1962)
Bristol City 4-1 Bristol Rovers (23/04/1963)

1963/1964
Division Three
Bristol City 3-0 Bristol Rovers (24/08/1963)
Bristol Rovers 4-0 Bristol City
(14/12/1963)

1964/1965
Division Three
Bristol Rovers 1-1 Bristol City (03/10/1964)
Bristol City 2-1 Bristol Rovers (13/02/1965)

1974/1975
Division Two
Bristol Rovers 1-4 Bristol City (28/12/1974)
Bristol City 1-1 Bristol Rovers (01/04/1975)

1975/1976
Division Two
Bristol City 1-1 Bristol Rovers (30/08/1975)
Bristol Rovers 0-0 Bristol City
(16/04/1976)

1980/1981
Division Two
Bristol City 0-0 Bristol Rovers (23/08/1980)
Bristol Rovers 0-0 Bristol City
(31/01/1981)

1981/1982
Division Three
Bristol Rovers 1-0 Bristol City (29/12/1981)
Bristol City 1-2 Bristol Rovers (12/04/1982)

1984/1985
Division Three
Bristol City 3-0 Bristol Rovers (10/11/1984)
Bristol Rovers 1-0 Bristol City
(13/04/1985)

1985/1986
Division Three
Bristol City 2-0 Bristol Rovers (29/03/1986)
Bristol Rovers 1-1 Bristol City (22/04/1986)

1986/1987
Division Three
Bristol City 0-1 Bristol Rovers (01/01/1987)
Bristol Rovers 0-0 Bristol City (18/04/1987)

1987/1988
Division Three
Bristol City 3-3 Bristol Rovers (12/09/1987)
Bristol Rovers 1-0 Bristol City (12/04/1988)

1988/1989
Division Three
Bristol City 0-1 Bristol Rovers (02/01/1989)
Bristol Rovers 1-1 Bristol City
(25/03/1989)

1989/1990
Division Three
Bristol City 0-0 Bristol Rovers (23/09/1989)
Bristol Rovers 3-0 Bristol City (02/05/1990)

1990/1991
Division Two
Bristol Rovers 3-2 Bristol City (26/01/1991)
Bristol City 1-0 Bristol Rovers
(05/03/1991)

1991/1992
Division Two
Bristol City 1-1 Bristol Rovers (04/09/1991)
Bristol Rovers 3-2 Bristol City
(21/12/1991)

1992/1993
Division One
Bristol Rovers 4-0 Bristol City (13/12/1992)
Bristol City 2-1 Bristol Rovers (06/04/1993)

1995/1996
Division Two
Bristol City 0-2 Bristol Rovers (16/01/1996)
Bristol Rovers 2-4 Bristol City (16/03/1996)

1996/1997
Division Two
Bristol City 1-1 Bristol Rovers (15/12/1996)
Bristol Rovers 1-2 Bristol City (16/03/1997)

1997/1998
Division Two
Bristol Rovers 1-2 Bristol City (04/11/1997)
Bristol City 2-0 Bristol Rovers (14/03/1998)

1999/2000
Division Two
Bristol City 0-0 Bristol Rovers (17/10/1999)
Bristol Rovers 2-0 Bristol City (22/04/2000)

2000/2001
Division Two
Bristol City 3-2 Bristol Rovers (22/12/2000)
Bristol Rovers 1-1 Bristol City (03/04/2001)

Cup Matches

1901
FA Cup
Bristol City 3-2 Bristol Rovers (27/11/1901)

1925
FA Cup
Bristol Rovers 0-1 Bristol City (10/01/1925)

1935
Division Three (South) Cup
Bristol City 4-2 Bristol Rovers (02/10/1935)

1945/1946
FA Cup
Bristol City 4-2 Bristol Rovers (08/12/1945)
Bristol Rovers 0-2 Bristol City (15/12/1945)

1957/1958
FA Cup
Bristol City 3-4 Bristol Rovers (15/02/1958)

1967/1968
FA Cup
Bristol City 0-0 Bristol Rovers (27/01/1968)
Bristol Rovers 1-2 Bristol City (30/01/1968)

1983/1984
FA Cup
Bristol Rovers 1-2 Bristol City (10/12/1983)

1984/1985
FA Cup
Bristol City 1-3 Bristol Rovers (08/12/1984)

1986/1987
Freight Rover Trophy
Bristol City 3-0 Bristol Rovers (16/12/1986)

1988/1989
Sherpa Van Trophy
Bristol Rovers 1-0 Bristol City (23/11/1988)

1991/1992
League Cup
Bristol Rovers 1-3 Bristol City (25/09/1991)
Bristol City 2-4 Bristol Rovers (08/10/1991)

1997/1998
League Cup
Bristol City 0–0 Bristol Rovers (12/08/1997)
Bristol Rovers 1-2 Bristol City (26/08/1997)

2001/2002
LDV Vans Trophy
Bristol City 3-0 Bristol Rovers (09/01/2002)

2006/2007
Johnstone's Paint Trophy Bristol City
0-0 Bristol Rovers (21/02/2007)
Bristol Rovers 1-0 Bristol City (27/02/2007)

Gloucester Cup

1898
Gloucester Cup
Bristol City 2-0 Bristol Rovers (26/02/1898)

1899
Gloucester Cup
Bristol City 2-1 Bristol Rovers (03/04/1899)

1900
Gloucester Cup
Bristol Rovers 1-1 Bristol City (02/04/1900)
Bristol City 1-0 Bristol Rovers (09/04/1900)

1901
Gloucester Cup
Bristol City 4-0 Bristol Rovers (29/04/1901)

1902
Gloucester Cup
Bristol Rovers 0-0 Bristol City (31/03/1902)
Bristol City 0-0 Bristol Rovers (23/04/1902)

1903
Gloucester Cup
Bristol Rovers 0-0 Bristol City (13/04/1903)
Bristol City 1-1 Bristol Rovers (20/04/1903)
Bristol City 2-4 Bristol Rovers (29/04/1903)

1904
Gloucester Cup
Bristol City 2-1 Bristol Rovers (04/04/1904)

1905
Gloucester Cup
Bristol Rovers 2-2 Bristol City(24/04/1905)
Bristol City 1-3 Bristol Rovers (28/04/1905)

1906
Gloucester Cup
Bristol City 4-0 Bristol Rovers (16/04/1906)

1907
Gloucester Cup
Bristol Rovers 0-2 Bristol City (01/04/1907)

1908
Gloucester Cup
Bristol City 2-0 Bristol Rovers
(29/04/1908)

1909
Gloucester Cup
Bristol Rovers 1-1 Bristol City (01/09/1909)
Bristol City 1-1 Bristol Rovers
(13/10/1909)

1910
Gloucester Cup
Bristol Rovers 1-2 Bristol City (26/01/1910)
Bristol City 2-0 Bristol Rovers
(06/04/1910)

1911
Gloucester Cup
Bristol Rovers 0-1 Bristol City (19/04/1911)

1912
Gloucester Cup
Bristol City 1-0 Bristol Rovers (03/02/1912)

1913
Gloucester Cup
Bristol Rovers 1-0 Bristol City (25/03/1913)

1914
Gloucester Cup
Bristol City 0-2 Bristol Rovers (14/04/1914)

1919
Gloucester Cup
Bristol Rovers 0-4 Bristol City (24/09/1919)

1920
Gloucester Cup
Bristol City 1-0 Bristol Rovers (29/09/1920)

1922
Gloucester Cup
Bristol Rovers 0-0 Bristol City (01/05/1922)

1923
Gloucester Cup
Bristol City 1-0 Bristol Rovers (07/05/1923)

1924
Gloucester Cup
Bristol Rovers 1-1 Bristol City (30/04/1924)
Bristol City 2-0 Bristol Rovers
(05/05/1924)

1925
Gloucester Cup
Bristol City 1-1 Bristol Rovers (27/04/1925)
Bristol Rovers 2-0 Bristol City
(29/04/1925)

1926
Gloucester Cup
Bristol Rovers 1-4 Bristol City (19/04/1926)

1927
Gloucester Cup
Bristol City 4-0 Bristol Rovers (01/01/1927)

1928
Gloucester Cup
Bristol Rovers 1-0 Bristol City (10/04/1928)
Bristol City 2-0 Bristol Rovers
(19/09/1928)

1929
Gloucester Cup
Bristol Rovers 0-0 Bristol City (30/09/1929)

1930
Gloucester Cup
Bristol City 4-1 Bristol Rovers (22/04/1930)
Bristol City 3-1 Bristol Rovers
(01/10/1930)

1931
Gloucester Cup
Bristol Rovers 0-1 Bristol City (09/09/1931)

1932
Gloucester Cup
Bristol City 3-3 Bristol Rovers (14/09/1932)

1933
Gloucester Cup
Bristol Rovers 3-4 Bristol City (24/04/1933)
Bristol Rovers 0-0 Bristol City (13/09/1933)

1934
Gloucester Cup
Bristol City 2-1 Bristol Rovers (03/04/1934)
Bristol City 1-2 Bristol Rovers
(26/09/1934)

1935
Gloucester Cup
Bristol Rovers 3-1 Bristol City (25/09/1935)

1936
Gloucester Cup
Bristol City 1-0 Bristol Rovers
(13/09/1936)

1937
Gloucester Cup
Bristol Rovers 2-1 Bristol City (27/09/1937)

1938
Gloucester Cup
Bristol City 3-0 Bristol Rovers (21/09/1938)

1945
Gloucester Cup
Bristol City 3-1 Bristol Rovers (24/09/1945)

1947
Gloucester Cup
Bristol Rovers 2-2 Bristol City (26/05/1947)
Bristol City 2-0 Bristol Rovers
(07/06/1947)

1948
Gloucester Cup
Bristol City 1-2 Bristol Rovers (08/05/1948)

1949
Gloucester Cup
Bristol Rovers 2-0 Bristol City (14/05/1949)

1950
Gloucester Cup
Bristol City 2-0 Bristol Rovers (13/05/1950)

1951
Gloucester Cup
Bristol Rovers 1-1 Bristol City (12/05/1951)

1952
Gloucester Cup
Bristol City 2-1 Bristol Rovers (10/05/1952)

1953
Gloucester Cup
Bristol Rovers 0-2 Bristol City (08/05/1953)

1954
Gloucester Cup
Bristol City 2-2 Bristol Rovers (03/05/1954)

1955
Gloucester Cup
Bristol Rovers 2-1 Bristol City (02/05/1955)

1956
Gloucester Cup
Bristol City 0-1 Bristol Rovers (02/05/1956)

1957
Gloucester Cup
Bristol Rovers 1-2 Bristol City (29/04/1957)

1958
Gloucester Cup
Bristol City 4-1 Bristol Rovers (29/04/1958)

1959
Gloucester Cup
Bristol Rovers 1-1 Bristol City (04/05/1959)

1960
Gloucester Cup
Bristol City 3-2 Bristol Rovers
(02/05/1960)

1961
Gloucester Cup
Bristol Rovers 1-3 Bristol City (01/05/1961)

1962
Gloucester Cup
Bristol City 3-1 Bristol Rovers (01/05/1962)

1963
Gloucester Cup
Bristol Rovers 2-1 Bristol City (23/05/1963)

1964
Gloucester Cup
Bristol City 2-2 Bristol Rovers (28/04/1964)

1965
Gloucester Cup
Bristol Rovers 3-2 Bristol City (26/04/1965)

1966
Gloucester Cup
Bristol City 0-1 Bristol Rovers (12/05/1966)

1967
Gloucester Cup
Bristol Rovers 0-3 Bristol City (09/05/1967)

1968
Gloucester Cup
Bristol City 1-1 Bristol Rovers (14/05/1968)

1969
Gloucester Cup
Bristol Rovers 0-5 Bristol City (28/04/1969)

1970
Gloucester Cup
Bristol City 2-1 Bristol Rovers (22/04/1970)

1971
Gloucester Cup
Bristol Rovers 1-1 Bristol City (04/05/1971)

1972
Gloucester Cup
Bristol City 1-1 Bristol Rovers (09/05/1972)

1973
Gloucester Cup
Bristol Rovers 2-2 Bristol City (01/05/1973)

1974
Gloucester Cup
Bristol City 0-2 Bristol Rovers (29/04/1974)

1975
Gloucester Cup
Bristol Rovers 2-1 Bristol City
(29/04/1975)

1976
Gloucester Cup
Bristol City 3-2 Bristol Rovers
(04/05/1976)

1977
Gloucester Cup
Bristol Rovers 0-1 Bristol City (24/05/1977)

1978
Gloucester Cup
Bristol City 3-0 Bristol Rovers (02/05/1978)

1979
Gloucester Cup
Bristol Rovers 0-2 Bristol City (15/05/1979)

1980
Gloucester Cup
Bristol City 1-0 Bristol Rovers (06/05/1980)

1981
Gloucester Cup
Bristol Rovers 0-1 Bristol City (05/05/1981)
Bristol City 0-1 Bristol Rovers
(08/09/1981)

1982
Gloucester Cup
Bristol Rovers 2-1 Bristol City (21/09/1982)

1983
Gloucester Cup
Bristol City 2-3 Bristol Rovers
(20/09/1983)

1984
Gloucester Cup
Bristol Rovers 3-1 Bristol City (21/05/1984)

1985
Gloucester Cup
Bristol City 1-0 Bristol Rovers (09/09/1985)

1987
Gloucester Cup
Bristol Rovers 1-2 Bristol City
(02/12/1987)

1988
Gloucester Cup
Bristol City 3-1 Bristol Rovers (15/03/1988)
Bristol Rovers 3-0 Bristol City (17/08/1988)

1989
Gloucester Cup
Bristol City 1-2 Bristol Rovers (08/08/1989)

1990
Gloucester Cup
Bristol Rovers 1-4 Bristol City (13/08/1990)

1991
Gloucester Cup
Bristol City 3-2 Bristol Rovers (17/08/1991)

1992
Gloucester Cup
Bristol Rovers 2-1 Bristol City (05/08/1992)

1993
Gloucester Cup
Bristol City 1-1 Bristol Rovers (05/08/1993)

1994
Gloucester Cup
Bristol Rovers 0-0 Bristol City (03/08/1994)

1996 **Gloucester Cup**
Bristol City 1-0 Bristol Rovers (17/08/1996)

Acknowledgements

I would like to thank my wife Sally for her support in the writing of this book and everything else I've ever done. My wonderful children, daughter Sophie and son Jack, who have made Sally and myself the proudest parents in the world.

My mum Maria for her support and in particular my dad Glyn who over many drinks with myself has talked endlessly about old footballers and how football used to be. I would also like to thank the rest of my family and my friends.

Thanks to Vanessa Gardner and all the staff at Green Umbrella. Vanessa, you believed in the book and for that I will always be grateful to you. Tom Hopgood for his support and his unbelievable knowledge of Bristol City Football Club. David Woods and Leigh Edwards, lads I couldn't have done it without you. Ed Furniss at Bristol City and Keith Brookman at Bristol Rovers. Darren Griffiths and Sue Palmer at Everton Football Club and Christine Stockton at Stoke City Football Club for their help and time and all the staff at Bristol Central Library which became my weekend residence.

And of course, all the players I have interviewed. I admired them as footballers before the book and after it, I admire them all as men. They were truly wonderful and some of them will be friends for life. I will be forever in their debt. They are all a credit to the blue or red shirt they wore.